FOR SON MAGNUS,

    THANKS FOR YOUR CONCERNS, RESPECT, CARING AND LOVE SHOWN ME OVER THE YEARS. I AM GLAD GOD BROUGHT ME IN YOUR LIFE. CONTINUE BEING A GOOD SON. I AM PROUD OF YOU. LOVE YOU!!!

Daddy,

[signature]

9/22/2015

The Retention
of First Year Black Male Students at Predominately White Private and Public Universities and Colleges

THE RETENTION
OF FIRST YEAR BLACK MALE STUDENTS AT PREDOMINATELY WHITE PRIVATE AND PUBLIC UNIVERSITIES AND COLLEGES

Dr. Sandy Woodrow Yancy, Sr.

The opinions expressed in this manuscript are solely the opinions of the author and do not represent the opinions or thoughts of the publisher. The author has represented and warranted full ownership and/or legal right to publish all the materials in this book.

The Retention of First Year Black Male Students at Predominately White Private and Public Universities and Colleges
All Rights Reserved.
Copyright © 2015 Dr. Sandy Woodrow Yancy, Sr.
v4.0

Cover Photo © 2015 Arnold Magnuss Wilson. All rights reserved - used with permission.
Interior images courtesy of Dr. Sandy Woodrow Yancy, Sr.

This book may not be reproduced, transmitted, or stored in whole or in part by any means, including graphic, electronic, or mechanical without the express written consent of the publisher except in the case of brief quotations embodied in critical articles and reviews.

Outskirts Press, Inc.
http://www.outskirtspress.com

ISBN: 978-1-4787-5574-6

Outskirts Press and the "OP" logo are trademarks belonging to Outskirts Press, Inc.

PRINTED IN THE UNITED STATES OF AMERICA

PREFACE

When I was growing up, my mother, the late Hannah Zeporah Pratt, always told me to finish what I started or 'don't start anything you can't finish.' Upon graduating from St. Patrick's High School on Capitol Hill, Monrovia, Liberia, I enrolled at the University of Liberia. After one semester I had to drop out due to financial reasons. I took two years off my college education to work and save some money so I could return. My mother again echoed her words of encouragement by repeating her advice about completing whatever I started. After the two years, I returned to complete my college education, receiving a Bachelor's Degree in Agriculture. After the graduation ceremony, she said to me, "You have finally finished what you started and I am happy for you." Her words of advice constantly resonated with me during my adult life. When I started my Master's Degree in Software Systems at the University of St. Thomas in St. Paul, Minnesota, her words of perseverance kept echoing in my ears. I completed my Master's Degree in Software Systems and was gratified to complete what I started. Later, I enrolled in the Doctorate of Educational Leadership program and completed that course of study at Argosy University, Washington, D.C. campus.

During my years at Argosy University and the University of St. Thomas, I concentrated seriously on retention. My dissertation topic was solely focused on the retention of first year Black male students at predominately White private universities or colleges. University of St. Thomas is a predominately White private Catholic university. During many of my classes, there were either two or three Black males. Most of the experiences we encountered are those that the participants are experiencing at this predominately White private university in the Washington, D.C. area. Both universities are offering opportunities to Black male students for completing their college degrees. I must commend these universities for their relentless efforts to render services to help educate Black males in the United States of America.

This book was solely written to provide evidence through my participants to prospective Black high school male graduates that want to attend predominately White private, White public universities or colleges. I wish my participants' experiences to somehow aid them in obtaining their college degrees. The education of Black males is important in the United States of America. The benefits derived from the education of Black males will improve their communities, provide financially for their families, enhance their self-esteem, and enable them to become valuable assets to their employers, and perhaps become business owners.

ABSTRACT

The purpose of this research was to obtain a better understanding about how to retain first year Black students at predominately White private institutions in light of Critical Race Theory Framework (CRTF). A retention model presented by Dr. Tinto was a focus in this study. Tinto's model is the most commonly referred model for student retention and for dropouts. Research questions were geared toward the pre-collegiate and collegiate experiences of three second semester freshmen and three sophomore Black male students at one predominately White private university in the Washington, D.C. area.

Qualitative, narrative research design was used in this study. The narrative aspect of the study dealt with the participants telling the stories of experiences that led to their success. Dr. Harper's Critical Race theory was used to better comprehend their stories related to race issues. Face-to-face interviews were conducted with each participant. All participants were in good academic standing and had completed at least 30 credits at this university. The stories collected from the participants enforced their willingness to become academically successful to obtain their various degrees. The interview guide questions focused on their pre-collegiate and collegiate experiences.

The eleven findings were drawn from pre-collegiate and collegiate experiences of the participants in achieving academic success. The major pre-collegiate findings were: a) positive interactions with high school teachers or guidance and mentors' assistance for college preparation, and b) parents and family members' encouragement and support to attend college. Major collegiate findings were a) involvement with retention programs on campus, b) social life on campus for Black male students, c) participation in leadership roles on campus, d) participation with mentoring programs on campus, e) student involvement, f) religion and spirituality, g) dealing with and overcoming frustration, h) determination to complete college and i) the importance of social networking on campus and the benefits for attending this predominately White private institution. From these eleven findings, only eight major themes answered the question: What conditions or factors contribute to the retention of first year Black male students at predominately White private institutions? The eight major themes that emerged from the study were: a) positive interactions with high school teachers or guidance and mentoring assistance for college preparation, b) parents and family members' encouragement and support to attend college, c) involvement with retention programs on campus, d) student involvement, e) religion and spirituality, f) dealing with and overcoming frustration on campus, g) determination to complete college and h) the appreciation of social network on campus and the benefits for attending this predominately White private institution.

The findings provided possible suggestions for high school seniors to utilize, for high school counselors to utilize, for College Student Affairs Administration to utilize, for faculty members to utilize and recommendations for further research for the academic success of first year Black male students at predominately White private universities and colleges.

DEDICATION

This research is dedicated to the loving memory of my mother; the late Hannah Zeporah Pratt, who as my late father, Seborn Nathaniel Yancy, said, showed us the school house doors, enabling us to become educated men and women. She has always been my role model. Although she has gone to her eternal rest, her advice about being educated always echoed in my ears. She instilled the fear of God in our hearts and reminded us that with God all things are possible. I admire her strength and faith in our Lord Jesus Christ.

ACKNOWLEDGEMENTS

My sincere thanks go to our Almighty God for giving me the strength and knowledge to complete this journey. I am walking in His plan for my life. He brought me from the Republic of Liberia, West Africa to the United States of America during the civil conflicts for a better and more prosperous life in this country. To God be the glory for all the wonderful things He has done and is continuously doing in my life.

To my wife, Magdalene Dennis Yancy, who has been my supporter on this journey through her constant reminders of God's presence on this journey and her tireless efforts in encouraging me to keep on progressing and not letting any distractions impair its completion. To my children who without any doubt told me that I can accomplish this pilgrimage. Thanks to Dr. Susan Crim for encouraging me to start my doctorate degree.

Thanks to my dissertation committee members: Dr. Joan Jackson, Dr. Farhad Khalatbari and Dr. George Fulda for their advices and support in helping me reach this milestone of my academic journey.

Thanks to all the participants for telling their stories about their academic success at a predominately White private university in the Washington, D.C. area. Their stories will be added to the literature to encourage other Black males graduating from high school that they can achieve academic success at a predominately White private institution if they are determined to put enough effort into achieving academic success. Thanks to this particular university for rendering various forms of assistance for the success of first year Black male students.

Thanks to my siblings for believing in my courage and determination to embark upon and accomplish this journey.

Thanks to all members of Mt. Zion United Methodist Church, Leesburg, Virginia for their prayers.

Table of Contents

PREFACE i
ABSTRACT iii
DEDICATION vii
ACKNOWLEDGEMENTS ix
CHAPTER 1: INTRODUCTION 1
    The Problem 3
    Problem Background 7
    The Purpose of the Study 13
    Research Questions 17
    Limitations 19
    Delimitations 21
    Definition of Terms 23
    Significance of the Study 25
    Research Method 31
    Theoretical Framework 33
    Summary 37

CHAPTER 2: LITERATURE REVIEW 39
   Minority at Predominantly White Institutions 41
   Student Engagement in Higher Education............................... 47
      Critical First Year Experience.. 48
      Masculinity 50
      Involvement.. 50
      Spirituality and Religion... 52
      Isolation 54
      Frustration.. 54
      Determination... 55
   Persistence in Higher Education 59
      Student Services 61
   Retention.. 63
   Mentoring 69
   Support Network... 73
   Theoretical Framework... 75
      Tinto's Model.. 76
      Critical Race Theory- Application by Shaun Harper........ 76
   Summary... 79

CHAPTER 3: METHODOLOGY.. 81
   Research Design.. 83
   Research Approach: Narrative study Approach 87
   Research Instrument 91
      Interviews... 92
   Population / Sampling 93
   Data Collection.. 95
      Interviews... 96
   Data Analysis Method 97
   Role of the Researcher.. 101
   Conclusion.. 103

CHAPTER 4: DATA ANALYSIS AND RESULTS 105
    Research Setting.. 107
    Background on Participants.. 109
    Data Collection.. 113
    Emerging Themes.. 115
    Pre-Collegiate Factors 119
        Theme 1: Positive Interactions with High School Teachers or Guidance and Mentors' Assistance for College Preparation 120
        Theme 2: Parents and Family members' Encouragement and Support to Attend College. 124
    Collegiate Factors 129
        Theme 3: Involvement with Retention Programs on Campus.. 130
        Theme 4: Social Life on Campus towards Black Male Students 132
        Theme 5: Participation in Leadership Roles on Campus.... 135
        Theme 6: Participation with Mentoring Programs on Campus 137
        Theme 7: Student Involvement... 139
        Theme 8: Religion and Spirituality... 142
        Theme 9: Dealing with and Overcoming Frustration..... 145
        Theme 10: Determination to Complete College 150
        Theme 11: The Importance of Social Network on Campus and the Benefits of Attending this Predominantly White Private Institution. 153
    Summary of Themes 163
    Conclusion.. 167

CHAPTER FIVE: DISCUSSION, CONCLUSIONS, IMPLICATIONS AND RECOMMENDATIONS 169
    Summary of the Study 171

Discussion of Findings 175
Pre-Collegiate Findings towards Academic Success 177
    Major Theme I: Positive Interactions with High School
    Teachers or Guidance and Mentors Assistance for
    College Preparation 178
    Major Theme II: Parents and Family members'
    Encouragement and Support to Attend College 179
Collegiate Findings towards Academic Success 181
    Major Theme III: Involvement with Retention
    Programs on Campus 182
    Major Theme IV: Student Involvement 182
    Major Theme V: Religion and Spirituality 183
    Major Theme VI: Dealing with and
    Overcoming Frustration 184
    Major Theme VII: Determination to Complete College 185
    Major Theme VIII: The Importance of Social
    Network on Campus and the Benefits for Attending
    this Predominantly White Private Institution 185
Perceptions from Participants 187
Conclusion 191
Implications for Practice 197
Suggestions for High School Counselors to Utilize 199
Suggestions for College Student Affairs Administrators
to Utilize 201
Suggestions for Faculty members to Utilize 207
Recommendations for Further Research 209
REFERENCES 217
APPENDICES 241

List of Tables

1. Black Students' Postsecondary Degree Attainment by Level and Sex, 2008 26
2. Background of Participants 110
3. Cross-Participant Analysis Display 154

List of Figures

1. Tinto's Model of Student Retention 33
2. Tinto's Model as Related to Study 35
3. Literature Review Graphical Illustration 78

List of Appendices

A. Introductory Script 243

B. Interview Guide: Dealing with Pre-Collegiate and
   Collegiate Factors 247

C. Alternative Consent Form For Research Containing
   Human Subjects 249

D. IRB Approval 255

E. Permission email from Dr. Vincent Tinto 259

CHAPTER 1:
INTRODUCTION

This is a phenomenological study that provided relevant information to conditions or factors that contributed to the retention of first year Black male students at predominately White private institutions. Research data looked at a private institution of higher learning located in the Washington, D.C. area. The topic is important because it provides evidence from the data collected to high school Black male senior students who want to attend predominately White private institutions (PWPI) to utilize as well as for high school counselors, college student affairs administration and faculty members to utilize. The problem area in the study was the academic accomplishments of first year Black male students at predominately White private institutions (PWPI), specifically their experiences and the key factors that contributed to their academic success. The study used the private university definition of students being in good academic standing (2.5) grade point average and above in determining academic success. Problems studied were academic performance, unwelcome environments, background of first year Black male students and spirituality.

The Problem

Nationwide, the Black student college graduation rate remains low, at 43% (The Journal of Blacks in Higher Education, 2009). Today, African American enrollment in higher education is at an all-time high. Although African American attendance is at an all-time high, there is still a 20-point gap in graduation as compared to Whites at 63% (The Journal of Blacks in Higher Education, 2009). This gap has enormous economic and societal implications. Houston best described the importance of educating African Americans as follows, "Without education, there is no hope for our people and without hope, our future is lost," (as cited in the Journal of Blacks in Higher Education, 2009, p. 1). There is an astonishingly significant difference between the number of African-American students who tend to start their college classes and those who actually end up graduating or completing their degree. During 2004, Black students acquired around 33 percent of the nation's bachelor's degrees (National Center for Education Statistics [NCES], 2006). The literature on college enrollment shows that Black men have the lowest enrollment rates of all college-aged students. By 2006, 37% of African American men of college age were enrolled at U.S. postsecondary institutions compared with 44.1% of White men (American Council on Education, 2006). In bachelor's degrees conferred, the gap between women and men widened. Sixty-one percent of bachelor's degrees awarded to Blacks in the 2000-01 academic years were earned by Black women (Harvey, 2003). The six-year graduation rate of Blacks in the 2000-01 academic years was 41 percent nationally, while White students posted a 61% graduation rate. Black women outpaced Black men by 11% (Harvey, 2003).

It was stated by Cuyjet (2006), that the decreasing number of Black male students on PWIs campus has another significant impact on the overall environment that influences everyone. A number of schools have agreed that they desire to have a diverse body of students, expecting that the members of the student body, administrators and faculty members within the campus community will, therefore, have an opportunity to learn and interact with each other intellectually, as well as culturally. There is an on-going debate about whether or not students coming from different cultural backgrounds should interact on PWIs campuses; even though, there are adequate numbers of students that have been coming from different ethnic backgrounds, for such types of interactions to take place, there must be sufficient amount of students in each of the demographics to represent their cultural groups (Decock, McCloy, Liu & Hu, 2011). Until we realize that there are significant cultural differences between African American women and men, specifically related to how they have been interacting with whites, we may tend to ignore the harmful effects and influences of the low number of African American men having the desired level of cultural interaction at the PWI campuses. Therefore, these issues must continuously be researched to add to the literature for the encouragement of the education of first year Black Male students at PWIs.

Problem Background

According to Harper and Davis (2012), perceptions about African American male underachievement and hopelessness are cited by a number of publications that highlight and identify their educational background in culturally unresponsive and insufficient K-12 institutions (Noguera, 2008; Toldson, 2008); their unpreparedness with respect to the strict and severe work at college level (Bonner & Bailey, 2006; Palmer & Young, 2009; Palmer, Davis, & Hilton, 2009); their lower rates of baccalaureate degree attainment (Dancy & Brown, 2008; Harper, 2006a, 2012; Strayhorn, 2010); their patterns of social and academic disengagement, outside and inside of the classroom environment (Kimbrough & Harper, 2006); and their lower rates of completing high school (Schott Foundation, 2010; Lynn et al., 2010). Furthermore, considerable efforts are exerted by African American male students throughout their educational levels in order to be perceived as cool and popular among their friends and peer groups (Stinson, 2006), and they must give as much importance to academic achievement as to athletic aspirations (Benson, 2000; Harper, 2009b). Even though, certainly a number of issues and problems are quantifiable and much has already been written about them, these tend to collectively communicate a message in public and academic discourse related to African American male students, and that is: they do not care much about education.

These explanatory issues and factors related to disinterest of African American male students in education have been mostly associated with educational and psychological outcomes (Milner, 2007; Jackson & Moore, 2008; Howard, 2008; Thomas & Stevenson, 2009). These are further used to describe the shortage of African American males who pursue their bachelor's degree in education and then acquire K-12 teaching as a profession (Shaw, 1996). It is noted in a report presented by Schott Foundation for Public Education in 2010 that only 47 percent of the African American male students have been graduated from high schools during 2008 with their peers becoming their cohorts. Consequently, degree attainment among the African American males at all post-secondary educational levels remains surprisingly and alarmingly low, specifically as compared to the female of the same race (see Table 1). Along with educational attainment contrast within their race, Black male students' representation in professional and graduate schools also remains behind their Asian American and Latino American male peers.

Under all these considerations, very little is understood about the African American male students who successfully manage to graduate from high schools, enroll in colleges, are motivated to earn / acquire degrees beyond the baccalaureate, espouse commitments to different career paths in educational and professional fields (education policy, teaching, education research, school administration, the professorate and so forth). What motivates particular Black male students to care so much about education and attaining a degree, in spite of continuous reports throughout the literature about generally being disengaged in schools and comparatively exhibiting a low rate of educational attainment? This question resulted in this research for gaining information about the experiences and perception of the retention of first-year Black male students at PWIs.

Table 1

Black Students' Postsecondary Degree Attainment by Level and Sex, 2008

	Men%	Women%
Associate's	31.4	68.6
Bachelor's	34.3	65.7
Master's	28.2	71.8
First Professional[1]	37.3	62.7
Doctoral[2]	33.6	66.4

[1] For example, J.D., M.D., and D.D.S. degrees
[2] Only Ph.D., Ed.D., and comparable doctoral degrees
Source: U.S. Department of Education (2010)

The African American male student enrollment in college campuses has emerged as a significant issue for PWIs during the previous forty to fifty years (Cross, 2002). This issue has attracted the attention of college administrators for investing more resources in new initiatives for recruiting and retaining Black male students from these minority populations by conducting orientation and mentoring programs, creating tutoring programs and providing funds for scholarships. Even though, a significant amount of progress is being made in this respect, yet African American males have continued to lag behind other minority populations in acquiring or attaining a college degree (The Chronicle of Higher Education Almanac, 2007).

Some Black communities once used to view education as a key aspect for living the American Dream. Now, many Black male students consider it as an unnecessary barrier or obstacle that stands in the way of making fast money. Generally, Black male students who manage to go to college, arrive at colleges unprepared for handling the requirements of higher educational institutions. Hamilton (1997) states that the reason behind this is that a significant number of Black male students who are college bound, arrived on campuses affected by consequences of previous interactions, associations and affiliations with adverse and severe socio-situational incidents that have emotionally wounded them.

As stated by Cureton (2009), problems and challenges such as lack of employment and education, discrimination, racial stereotyping, economic deprivation and exploitation have significantly affected the self-esteem, personal confidence and social development of Black male students. This also negatively influences young generations of Black male students who are looking forward to somehow enhance their chances in life in respect to social status, prestige, power and wealth.

The Purpose of the Study

As stated by Kanpp, Kelly-Reid and Whitmore (2006) there is a need to understand the issues that shape the academic success of African American students at every level of higher education. There is particular interest in the necessity of obtaining a better insight of Black students' experiences predominantly at White Institutions (PWIs), where most of the Black students are now gaining admissions and receiving their academic education.

Despite depressing achievement data which was measured by the grade point average based on the achievement gap between the Black and White, it was observed that Black students tend to be successful in spite of the obvious odd situations (Corwin & Pruitt, 2000). The purpose of this research was to obtain a better understanding about how to retain the first year Black students at predominantly White private institutions under the light of Critical Race Theory Framework (CRTF). In a study conducted by Harper (2009), a methodological approach was performed which was popularized by theorists of critical race. This approach was used for opposing dominant dialogues and arguments that were concerned with the educational and social status of Black male students in America. Particularly, this counter argument on the achievement of students was derived by having individual, face-to-face interviews with 143 Black male students in around 30 predominantly White universities and colleges all across America.

A retention model presented by Tinto was focused on in this study. Tinto's model is the most commonly referred model for student retention and dropouts. According to Tinto (1975), the basic idea of his model is the integration. The model claims that the attitude of whether a student drops out or remains is significantly predicted by the extent to which these students are socially integrated and academically integrated. These behaviors evolve over the passage of time, as commitment and integration interact with the rate of students dropping out as depending upon the level of commitment while decision making. These might be measured through: personal development, grade/ marks performance and academic integration.

According to Tinto's model, students tend to enter the college or university with individual as well as family attributes and characteristics, along with the pre-college schooling attributes. They enter into an environment or a system which is characterized by intellectual development and grade performance, and it collectively leads the student toward academic integration, entering a social system where faculty interaction and peer interaction further lead the students toward social integration. Social and academic integration work together to affect the institutional commitments and on-going goals. This consequently leads the students to decide whether they want to leave or stay at the college. Later, this model was revised by adding commitment related to intentions to remain within the college or dropping out of the institution.

Research Questions

Qualitative inquiry involves systematic collection, organization, and interpretation of material derived from speech and observation (Creswell, 2009). This study was guided by the central research question: **What conditions or factors contribute to the retention of first year Black male students at predominantly White private institutions?** In order to gain an understanding of academic success, it was important to have sub-questions related to campus involvement, social life, and cultural identity that contribute to retention. The interview protocol questions are located in the Appendix. The sub-research questions for pre-college factors and in-college factors are as follows: For pre-college factor - What are the factors that influence the Black students' pre-college experiences? For in-college factor - How did the experiences of Black male students assist in achieving retention success at Predominantly White Private Institutions (PWPI)? Literature has found that these questions are necessary to understand the retention of Black male students at predominantly White private institutions.

LIMITATIONS

A limitation of the study was the purposive sampling that was used for first year Black male students. The results of this study provided a mere description of factors that have contributed to the retention of first year Black male students at predominantly White private institutions (PWPI). Merriam (2012) states "results would be limited to describing the phenomenon rather than predicting future behavior" (p.41). Also, the social climate for Black male students varies from campus to campus, as well as the availability and the quality of supportive resources. Depending on the college or university, support programs such as tutoring, progressive multicultural centers, and the opportunity to attend cultural awareness programs vary. Therefore, these factors could impact academic success. Lastly, the findings of this research were limited to a degree as these findings and conclusions were made upon one set of interpretations presented by the researcher about one set of data related to the academic success of Black male students. Also, the study was limited to one predominantly White private institution in the Washington, D.C. area.

Delimitations

The only participants who were eligible for this study were first year second semester and sophomore Black male undergraduate students at one predominantly White private institution in the Washington, D.C. area. Second semester first year Black male students have completed 18 credits and sophomore Black male students have completed 36 credits and include both those who are in good academic standing as well as students who are at risk for drop-out. Therefore, transfer students were not eligible.

Definition of Terms

Black: Black is any person having a known ancestry to Africa, South America or the Caribbean (Smith, 2010).

PWI: Predominantly White institutions are universities or colleges where the majority of the population of students is White (Smith, 2010).

HBCU: Historically Black colleges and universities are higher education institutions specifically established to educate African Americans (Smith, 2010).

HBI: An historically Black institution is a higher education institution specifically established to educate African Americans (Smith, 2010).

Academic Success: Academic success means an individual has successfully surpassed his or her goals or a set GPA. It involves ability to communicate with others, analyze and interpret information correctly, leading projects through to completion, and self-motivated decision-making skills (Smith, 2010).

Retention: Retention is often operationalized as the percentage of first-time, full-time students returning to the same institution for their second year of college" (Mattern & Patterson, 2009, p. 1).

Attrition: It is a reduction in the number of students enrolling or re-enrolling and the reduction in the population of students because of increased dropouts or transfers (Smith, 2010).

Persistence: a decision of students to retain or stay within the university or college enrollment (Smith, 2010).

Experience: This concept entails the accumulation of knowledge or skill that results from observation or direct participation in events or activities (Picket, 2000).

Involvement: The amount of energy and time that college students devote to participating in clubs and organizations, studying, interacting with faculty and peers, spending time on campus, and utilizing campus facilities. It occurs when a student psychologically invests in learning new things (Smith, 2010).

Significance of the Study

The significance of the study was designed to provide research on a problem that is important to colleges and universities, society, and Black male students who will enter college. Colleges and universities could benefit from this study because it has examined the experiences that shape the success of Black males. According to Harper (2005), over half of Black students who enroll in college do not complete their degrees. On a societal level, the lack of Black males attaining their degrees decreases their earning and political power. The lack of academic success and degree attainment over time potentially affects the community status, family relationships and leadership roles.

For Black males, the findings of this study have provided empowerment and confidence in obtaining academic success. Becoming aware of the factors that lead to academic success as well as the obstacles, Black male students can control their overall college experience and become insightful student leaders contributing to the overall campus student body. Finally, the study findings have possibly provided insight into what factors help to facilitate academic success for Black males. These findings could potentially make a positive contribution to helping high school teachers, college administrators, and faculty members address academic success for Black males.

Furthermore, the results and findings of the study should be beneficial in informing the higher education policymaker and administration in their effort to develop a better understanding, as well as in identifying different aspects in which campus administrators can design their mentoring programs for Black male students at predominantly White private institutions. The research significance has provided information of retention challenges for minority students at PWIs, so that the higher education commission can expand its research base and provide assistance to policymakers in designing effective mentoring programs with the help of Black male students who have successfully persevered and achieved higher academic performance. This study also has a chance for contributing at large to sociological perspectives that are related to the role and responsibilities of social institutions in creating and maintaining the equality forms. This could be done by identifying how social institutions contributed to creating systems of inequality through racial discrimination and racial grouping in PWIs.

Results in this study were compared to studies such as:

1. Harper (2004) *The Measure of a Man: Conceptualizations of masculinity among High-Achieving African American male college students.* Harper findings indicated that unconventional definitions of masculinity, when coupled with active campus involvement and leadership in minority student organizations, are deemed acceptable by uninvolved undergraduate men and help promote healthy masculine identities for African American male student leaders.

2. Smith (2010) *A Study of how predominantly white institutions of higher education in Indiana address retention and graduation rates of African American students.* The Smith study used qualitative methodology. In his review of literature on K-12 and HBCU's strategies, these assisted him in developing interview questions that were used to identify practices in retaining and graduating African American students in PWIs in the Midwest. Ten participants from PWIs participated in the telephone interviews to identify common and / or unique practices as compared to the literature.

3. Sinanan (2012) *Still Here: African American Male Perceptions of Social and Academic Engagement at a 4-Year, Predominantly White Institution of Higher Learning in Southern New Jersey.* The Sinanan study explored perceptions of the academic, social, and institutional forces that shape success for African American male students attending a 4-year, predominantly White public college in Southern New Jersey. The study utilized an interview-based qualitative research method to examine African American male students' social

and academic experiences at a small, predominantly White, liberal arts college in southern New Jersey.

4. Chesson (2009) *Brother To Brother: A narrative inquiry of African American male experiences of academic success at Colorado State University*. Chesson's study used a qualitative, narrative inquiry research design. Narrative inquiry enabled Chesson to learn from the participants through storytelling. Critical Race Theory (CRT), an emerging theory in the field of education, was used to better understand the stories and the impact of race for African American male students. In-depth interviews were conducted using a purposeful sample of six African American male students, who were in good academic standing and completed at least 60 credits, while attending Colorado State University. The narratives collected from the interviews provided a voice for the participants' perceptions of what it took to become academically successful.

5. George (2011) *Perceptions of African-American Males on Retention: Two Focus Groups. The George study was of two small focus groups comprised of African-American students of various grade classifications from a regional comprehensive university in the southeast.* These focus groups were comprised of up to but no more than six students. The decision on the group size was made to allow all of the students' ample opportunity to respond to the eight questions used in the focus groups. Various themes emerged as a result of this study which includes: importance of family support prior to college and during the students' college career.

6. Bowie (2006) *Using Multivariate logistic regression and analysis to predict Black male student persistence at a predominantly white institution: An approach investigating the relationship between engagement and persistence.* The Bowie study examined the impact of student engagement on persistence decisions of Black males attending a predominantly White public institution in the South. Bowie study was designed to empower Black males attending Kappa University

and to encourage them to take more of a commanding role in their persistence. Persistence of Black males is multidimensional and requires support from family, community, faculty, peers and administrators. The finding of the study identified the importance of student engagement on persistence decisions of Black males attending Kappa University.

This study is different from other studies in that it presented a certain demographic of participants who are second semester freshmen and sophomores who are academically successful at White private institutions. This study was geared toward a specific sampling of participants. An understanding of the persistence in retention in the initial two years of college at predominantly White private institutions for Black male students was examined. Themes that were obtained from this study are definitely beneficial to colleges, universities, Black male students, family and the community. Further research is needed to provide ample literature in the retention of first year Black male students at predominantly White private institutions.

Research Method

This study employed a qualitative narrative approach. Qualitative research has been defined by Creswell (2009) as a process of investigating and enquiring regarding understandings based on distinctive methodological traditions yielding discoveries which help in exploring a human or social problem. Qualitative research will involve collecting data from participants in their natural setting. It operates on the assumption that action can best be understood when it is observed in the setting that it occurs. Researchers carrying on qualitative studies are usually interested in developing an understanding of the meaning people construct--for instance, how they conceive meaning out of their world and the experiences that they have in their lives (Merriam, 2012, p. 6).

The researcher believes that in the marginalization issues, the stories that have been told by the people who have experienced and lived it are more valid, meaningful and powerful as compared to statistics and numbers. Furthermore, the researcher believes that quantitative research helps in understanding the "what" of the research questions, and is essential for research investigation; whereas qualitative research explains to us the "why" part of the study, concerned with understanding why something is happening. Specifically, why do first year Black male students at predominantly White private institutions experience academic success?

THEORETICAL FRAMEWORK

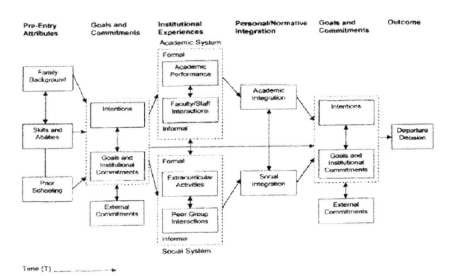

Figure 1. Tinto's Model of Student Retention
(Source: Audrey, Jaeger and Eagan, 2009)

Permission to use Tinto's Model of Student Retention was granted by email on January 7, 2014. Kindly see Appendix E.

Dr. Tinto's model of retention, along with critical race theory by Dr. Shaun Harper, were used in this study as the theoretical framework. Tinto's student retention model (1987, 1993, 2000, 2006), is the most comprehensive model that is being used by researchers for developing their theoretical framework and foundation of their study. The model involves all the factors, starting from pre-entry attributes to goals and commitment of an individual, institutional experiences, personal/ normative integration and the outcome (in terms of whether the individual decides to remain in the institution or will leave). The in-college factors in Tinto's model are usually measured via two different categories: *Academic Integration*: personal development based on the students' personal judgment about how they value the things they are learning (in opposition to the marks given by teachers and their judgments); *Academic-self-esteem-* understanding whether they are enjoying their subjects and enjoy studying them by analyzing their perception about the study patterns and formats, their identification with academic values and norms, and how they identify their role and responsibilities as students, including grade and marks performances. *Social Integration*: Number of friends they have-where it probably does not matter whether they fit in with a dominating social crowd or group. What matters is whether they have a group of friends where they fit in or not. Personal contacts with administrators or academics- it might be possible to measure a small number of contacts, number of staff personnel they know, how many staff members smile at them, number of staff personnel they personally tend to interact with even if it is small, whether they enjoy being on the campus or not, etc.

This research used the retention model along with critical race theory in order to develop the theoretical framework for the study.

INTRODUCTION 35

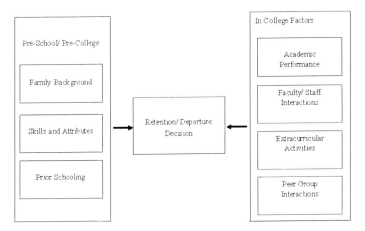

Figure 2. Tinto's Model as related to study

Harper's Critical Race Theory Application (2012). A study conducted by Harper (2009) adopted a methodological approach which was based on the critical race theorists which were used for opposing the dominant discourse related to the educational and social status of Black students in the U.S. In this manner, the study used the critical race theory in order to analyze the experiences of Black men and provided them a platform through which they could easily share their pre-college and in-college experiences and how they have been successful in dealing with the challenges for successful retention. The main intention was to allow these men to voice their experiences and to provide insights on how to enhance their academic success at this predominantly White private institution.

Summary

Research data looked at one of the predominantly White private institutions located in Washington, D.C. areas. The following presents: population and sampling, instrumentation, data collection activities and data analysis procedure. For population/sampling, participants were selected from second semester freshmen and sophomores. Although it is important to focus on themes and structures articulated by the participants, the researcher scrutinized nonverbal communication and meanings that are less conscious (interpersonal space, body movement, posture, volume, and pitch (Fontana & Frey, 2008). In light of the various recommendations mentioned in the review of literature section, the researcher focused on themes related to the academic success of Black male students at predominantly White private institutions. Throughout the process, the researcher engaged with the literature, and where new themes emerged, the researcher sought after relevant research.

Chapter two was presented with the literature review dealing with literature collected on major areas as explored in this research. They are retention with sub-titles of masculinity, mentoring and involvement. Religion and spirituality along with isolation, frustration, determination and support network were discussed to justify the findings of literature to support this study. A graphical illustration of chapter 2 was presented to further explain in detail the significance of literature represented that was beneficial to first year Black male students for obtaining academic success at predominantly White private institutions.

CHAPTER 2:
LITERATURE REVIEW

Minority at Predominantly White Institutions

A majority of the literature published regarding Black males is offered from a deficit perspective. During the 1980s, the number of Black students living in the college dorms was approximately equal to the people who were in prison. These statistics are startling to the growth of the Black community. Bailey & Moore (2004) identified Black males being viewed as a population at risk in education, and described this with words that have negative connotations such as 'uneducable, endangered, dysfunctional, dangerous, and lazy' as a big challenge that impacts enrollment for these students. Using such words to identify Black males can perpetuate stereotypes among educators, and this can become self-threatening to Black men (Bailey & Moore, 2004).

The Black male students' collegial outcomes and experiences, in regard to a successful discussion of the post-secondary educational system, are not understood completely. Black male students have generally been observed to be successful when Black men have been provided opportunities to participate and seek higher education, along with formalized, well-conceived and well-designed support systems being available in order to promote students' achievement (Richards, 2007). Richards (2007) found that parental involvement, encouragement from mentors, and positive experiences in school were factors that led to the success of Black male students.

Research on the experiences of Black male students at predominantly White universities (PWIs) and Historically Black Colleges & Universities (HBCUs) is scattered amongst the literature. This study has provided voice to a small population that is often neglected or misinterpreted. Black males have a story to tell about their academic experience that is uniquely their own. It is likely different from that of their white colleagues and dissimilar to Black women. In order to add to the limited published literature, this study has researched the factors that led to the academic success of first year Black male students enrolled at one White private institution in the

Washington, D.C. area. Chesson (2009) conducted a similar study at Colorado State University focusing on the perceived factors related to academic success of African American males on a predominantly white campus. Chesson (2009) found that cohesiveness and solidarity of African American males, alienation and isolation, and negative attitudes toward White students fostered feelings of resentment. Family support and role models were key factors influencing the academic success of African American males. Chesson's (2009) study has provided insight into factors of academic success for African American males at predominantly white institutions.

According to the U.S. Department of Education (2009), the graduation rates for Black males in colleges and universities are declining; universities and colleges need to formulate a program to assist the first year Black males to stay in college and obtain their degrees. Continuing sophomores in large portion are good signs of an effective retention program. As stated by Harper (2006), first year Black males have a tremendous challenge, especially in attending predominantly white institutions. Typical experiences they encounter are isolation, culture shock and frustration. However to get through distracted atmospheres such as isolation, culture shock and frustration, they involve themselves in spiritual guidance and determination. Spiritual guidance means believing in a supreme power to help them achieve their educational goals. By being determined, they are able to join forces with other Black male students and develop a networking environment to succumb to the negative atmosphere surrounding their distraction at such institutions.

According to Harper (2006), first year Black male students at predominantly white institutions must realize the environment they are placed in and must learn to communicate with their faculty members, administrative staff, and admission counselors. They must join some support group. Faculty, on the other hand, must be supportive in eliminating the racial tension in class and on campus.

Faculty support, advising, and extra curricular activities are important for retention. First year Black males at PWI are sensitive to any distraction because they have been in the minority in society and coming to such an institution reinforces societal classification. According to Jackson and Moore (2008), faculty support must extend far beyond advising, since faculty members are the persons in constant contact with the students, their concerns for student grades, well-being, inquiring about personal situations, having an open door policy and equal time for both Black and white students are paramount in the retention of Black males at a predominantly white institution. When Black students sense an atmosphere of equal time with white students, they develop self-confidence and realize that they are important to their faculty members. Since there are more white institutions than Black, the enrollment of Black students to white universities will always be in large portion. First year Black males, on the other hand, are a smaller population than first year Black females enrolling at predominantly white institutions. Therefore, the psychological state of Black males is disturbing, making them feel not worthy to be in competition with females of their own race. However, the retention of all first year Black males leading to graduation is important for the education of Black males.

For example, Furr (2002) examined the factors that promote persistence to degree completion at PWIs. The findings from Furr's (2002) study stated that African American students' retention rate in the first semester at the institution was 97% compared to 92% of White students. However, the retention rates for African American students dropped to 68% after four semesters at the PWI compared to 72% White students. Furr's (2002) study reported a strong correlation between positive multicultural experiences and African American retention rate. The findings from Furr's (2002) study argue that persistence factors of African American students at PWIs are dependent upon prior and early university experiences. At the conclusion of her study, Furr (2002) also recommended that higher education administrators and policy makers become aware of the warning signs of student attrition when working with African American students.

Although significant strides have been made to increase African American accessibility to postsecondary institutions, there is a significant gap between the academic performance and degree attainment of African Americans and their White counterparts (Davis, Palmer & Hilton, 2009). Davis (2008) believes that the academic achievement gap is determined and attributed to the pathways that African American students take to get to postsecondary institutions and their ability to navigate through various academic pathways. These pathways have created challenges for higher education administrators and policymakers. Due to the increased accountability pressures, scholarly practitioners have been summoned to reconstruct their institutions in order to address the changing demographics of their student populations. Although significant strides have been made to increase African American accessibility to postsecondary institutions, there is a significant gap between the academic performance and degree attainment of African Americans and their White counterparts (Davis, 2008). Davis (2008) believes that the academic achievement gap is determined and attributed to the pathways that African American students take to get to postsecondary institutions and their ability to navigate through various academic pathways. These pathways have created challenges for higher education administrators and policymakers. Due to the increased accountability pressures, scholarly practitioners have been summoned to reconstruct their institutions to address the changing demographics of their student populations.

Student Engagement in Higher Education

Student engagement in higher education presents an area of research and focus for colleges and universities. The most accepted definition of student engagement involves efforts and time that are devoted by students in activities as associated to their collegial outcomes, and what colleges and universities have been doing in order to induce students to participate in various activities (Kuh, 2009). Others have defined student engagement more loosely as an indicator of institutional excellence (Axelson & Flick, 2011).

CRITICAL FIRST YEAR EXPERIENCE

This study was aimed at learning from first year Black male students their experiences at one predominantly White private university to provide a deeper understanding of these experiences, through which a discussion about the first year of college was provided. The first year of college is the most crucial time period for most students (Barefoot, 2000). During this time students are making the transition from high school to higher education, and they are adjusting to both new found freedoms and increased responsibilities (Gardner & Barnes, 2007). During the first year of college students are learning how to coexist with their roommate(s), while trying to keep up with the quick pace of their college classes. The first year is not only a critical time for adjustment to college, it is also the time in which students decide to stay or depart from college. It is the time when students decide if they have made the right decision. They are observing whether they have chosen the right college for them, and they are deliberating whether college is for them at all (Tinto, 1987; Upcraft, Barefoot, 2000; Gardner & Barnes, 2007) and many are leaving.

Barefoot (2000) suggested that administrators have continued to be frustrated and disappointed with significantly higher rates of college dropout rate from college between their first year and second year. She suggests that one reason for this pervasive and high dropout rate is due to our current way of framing the issues (Kidwell, Blair, Hardesty, Childers, 2008). She suggests if you ask most college faculty what's wrong with the first college year, they will zoom in on the deficiencies of the students. They may lament that new students are not engaged academically, they can't write, they are unmotivated to learn and they expect instant gratification. In short, they aren't the students of the glory days. She further states that college-goers have changed in a number of significant ways since the time when most current faculty were themselves undergraduates. Researchers estimate that over the next two decades 65 percent of the population growth in the United States will be within those groups labeled "minority," such as Black, Latino, Asian and Native American. Thus, there will be an increased presence of diversity on campus and in the classrooms (Kidwell, Blair, Hardesty, Childers, 2008). And yet, the dominant structure of the first college year is the same basic college structure that was designed for a population of white, middle-or upper-class males, who constituted the vast majority of college students until the last two decades of this century and began to change after WWII. For many of today's new students, there is a serious lack of institutional fit, not of their making.

In an effort to increase the likelihood of institutional fit, colleges and universities have developed first-year initiatives. Although, these initiatives differ in their development and execution, they do share some of the same research-based goals: 1) increasing the expectations of academic engagement at the educational level; 2) helping out students who do not have a sufficient amount of academic preparation for meeting the college criteria; 3) increasing interactions between students and faculty; 4) increasing interactions between students, themselves; 5) increasing the time spent at campus and students' involvement on the campus; and 6) creating a link between curriculum and the co-curriculum.

Masculinity

According to Harper (2009), African American students often characterized masculinity into two different categories or orientations: "player for women" and "tough guy." They relate tough guys to be the ones who are good at fighting, incite fear in others and are never afraid when it comes to defending themselves. In their view, the concept of players of women is usually more prevalent during the young adulthood and teenage years, and is often associated with being tough. They consider players to be those who have multiple sexual partners and girlfriends. Those people who are not capable and unsuccessful in achieving these aims and goals are usually made fun of, are considered less masculine than their peers, or have their heterosexuality questioned. A research conducted by Dancy (2009) studied Black manhood in colleges. Black male students in colleges experience pressure in fulfilling media-related social expectations to be aggressive, athletic and overly sexual in college. The research unearthed hidden issues and pressures faced by Black male students across twelve different colleges for fulfilling social expectations to be overly sexual, overly aggressive, and athletic in college. A majority of the participants from this study suggested or claimed that the aggressive, stereotypical and dominant images of Black students in colleges represented by media, specifically in movies and televisions, has been one of the most prominent reasons for the increased pressure at college or university.

Involvement

It is stated by Harper (2006) that involvement is considered to be one of the key aspects for the success of Black male students at the collegial level. His study examines the gains (benefits) and outcomes (results) that are connected with outside class activities, especially experiences related to leadership. The researcher has reviewed previous studies and has discussed current trends of involvement. This research analyzed how involvement, which is defined by Smith (2010) as the amount of energy and time that college students devote to participating in clubs and organizations, studying, interacting with faculty and peers, spending time on campus, and utilizing campus facilities. It occurs when a student psychologically invests in learning new things. This research suggests that the involvement benefits are linked with the degree to which a student is capable of connecting in-class learning with that of their experiences gained outside the classroom. Involvement of students in these types of activities tends to influence their leadership and learning within the organization. It has further depicted a positive impact on problem solving and critical thinking, along with their motivation and preparedness for post-baccalaureate activities.

It is further stated by Harper (2012) that trends of involvement among the Black male undergraduate students indicate that very few of these students tend to engage and involve in activities outside the class in predominantly White institutions. Harper (2012) also stated that the gap in enrollment of Black male and female students is increasing, where male students have been withdrawing from the leadership positions in huge numbers. Through this research, Harper presented the self-reported gains and benefits for the Black male students, who get highly involved, and the privileges and the perks of becoming involved in campus leadership activities.

Furthermore, it is reported by Harper (2009) that engaged and involved students tend to now equal the socio-economic progression projected in the future. If we place greater emphasis for retaining and engaging African American male students at present, then we would eventually be able to increase the number of Black male students acquiring bachelor's degrees in the United States of America. This has been highlighted as significant for reducing the socio-economic gap between the White and the Black students.

Approximately twenty years back, it was stated by Perry and Locke (1985, p. 107) that Black men have higher unemployment, lower median income, and are usually employed at less prestigious positions as compared to White men. In 2004, Shapiro found that on average White men tend to earn significantly greater than Black men do, with comparable and competing educational credentials. The average yearly salary earned by White men having a bachelor's degree was $ 51,099 in 2000, whereas the Black men having bachelors' degrees earned $40,360 on average (National Center for Education Statistics [NCES], 2003). The reason behind this gap is the disparity among the Black and White men. These findings and observations have validated the assertions made by Gordon, Gordon and Nembhard (1994):

> *"Africa American male professionals have continued to be excluded out from leadership positions, are often considered to be incapable of handling technical work or management, thus, they continue to earn lesser than their White male counterparts" (P. 518).*

Therefore, it has become increasingly important to expose the African American male undergraduates and to avail them of opportunities which will help in strengthening their likelihood to attain a bachelor's degree and to become capable, thus successfully competing for rewarding jobs after graduating from college.

SPIRITUALITY AND RELIGION

According to research conducted by Watson (2006), religion and spirituality in lives of Black men in college are topics which are rarely covered by authors and researchers. In his research, Watson (2006) has presented practical definitions of both religion and spirituality. According to his definitions, spirituality is a belief in some animating, external force and religion is adhering to an established system of practices and beliefs grounded under spirituality. Both religion and spirituality have been playing a significant part in the way African American male college students perceive their responsibilities. Watson identified and analyzed the role played by spirituality in African American male students' lives and how it can be used for developing their identity and helping them to develop their coping skills throughout their college experience. Watson reviewed several perspectives related to spirituality, considering them under a framework of daily practices for Black people. Watson's study was conducted consisting of 97 first year and second year Black male college-going students. The information was obtained about the students' religious and spiritual beliefs and their educational/academic experiences. It was revealed in the findings that through religious activities, spirituality was significant to these students and to achieving their purpose in life. Most of the students were observed to identify one special person in their lives that is critical and important for their survival and their success. These students also believed that whatever obstacle appears in their way, they can handle it with the grace of a higher being.

The students were also observed to illustrate the concept of *"resistant soul force"* presented by C.F Stewart (1999) which helps an individual to thrive, to survive and to overcome human oppressions. It was also concluded by Steward that in number of higher educational institutions, religion and spirituality are not encouraged and affirmed by the professionals and teachers at college, although these concepts can help in positively influencing the identity development of Black male students. Spirituality and religion has always been a key in the lives of Black women and men. Believing in spiritual powers has given them comfort to deal with any situations that seem unbearable and must be dealt with to overcome their hardships.

Isolation

A survey research conducted by Loo & Rollison(1986) focusing on White and minority undergraduates observed and highlighted that a higher level of minority alienation must be assessed. Factors which help in reducing alienation such as social acceptance of minority groups, leadership positions, encouragement in classroom activities are highlighted and similarities and differences between perceptions of White and minorities about the ethic representation and clustering are ascertained.

Suen (1983) conducted a study and suggested that programs designed to reduce alienation should focus on the reduction of social estrangement, while programs designed to reduce attrition should focus on reduction. Isolation is a serious problem at predominantly white institutions when it comes to accepting Black male students into their environment. Black male students are not easily accepted into the social lives of white students. This phenomenon increases the isolation of Black students on campus. The literature obtained for this concept explained the reduction of alienation focused on social estrangement as opposed to the appreciation of ethnicity.

Frustration

As stated by Delgado (1998), predominantly White institution models deal with the individuals who were academically capable of meeting the standards set by Whites. For example those with standard test scores and high-grade point averages are typically people who have assimilated culturally into the mainstream/limelight of the society and these are also the people who have the financial resources to pay for the increasing costs of education. Consequently, any individual who does not meet the standards set by the tenets of the dominating paradigm in America might have to struggle significantly at the White institutions. This has led to an increasing emotion of frustration which turns out to be detrimental for Black male students at PWIs. By removing the standards created by Whites, for example high academic scores, test scores and high-grade averages, accepting those Black male students who have a financially strong background, can help in easing the situations and frustration faced by the Black male students at PWIs.

DETERMINATION

The research conducted by Howard-Hamilton (1997) explored some of the developmental theories which could be adopted in order to fit the needs of Black male students. The study also analyzed new theories that are Afro-centric and might prove to be helpful in improving the experiences of Black men and promoting self-esteem. The study has made an effort to present a practical application of the selected theories by analyzing them. The researcher has argued that graduate faculty and practitioners need to have developmental theories that correspond accurately to the problems that are faced by Black students (Lynn, Bacon, Totten, Bridges & Jennings, 2010). Furthermore, the study depicted that these theories can be translated into practical applications for enhancing learning outcomes. After critiquing and reviewing the traditional developing theories, Howard-Hamilton (1997) provided a model which includes additional dimensions focusing on different issues such as interaction, spirituality, affiliation, social responsibility, interdependence, identity and awareness before the application of any traditional developmental theories to Black male students.

Furthermore, the study reviewed four various theoretical frameworks that could be employed in addressing problems particularly related to Black male students: 1) Robinson and Howard-Hamilton's Afrocentric Resistance Model (1994); 2) Cross's Nigrescence Theory (1991, 1995); 3) Bandura's Social Learning

Model (1977); and 4) Erikson's Identity Development Model (1980). Cross developed Nigrescence Theory (1991, 1995) which was a five phase developmental theory of acquiring Black identification.

He named this theory Nigrescence which means a process of becoming Black. These five-phases were: Pre-encounter, Encounter, Immersion, Emersion and Internalization. The initial stage refers to the time when an individual is unaware of his or her race, or many times the racial implications. The second stage is referred to the time when racial awareness occurs for the first time. This phase many times occurs earlier in one's lifetime among the racial minorities as compared to the advantaged group or racial majority (usually explained as superior group). At this stage, the moment comes when an individual--as a teenager or as a child-has been treated differently or discriminatingly because he or she has a different color. In the third stage, a person realizes and takes on all the identified elements of his or her race. During this phase, an individual being a strong member of his or her group, embraces all the characteristics, features and behaviors that are linked with being a member of that racial group. In the fourth phase, an individual comes out to find different characteristics, features and behaviors that they might admire and want to adopt from other racial groups. At this stage, one becomes socially comfortable with other groups and values relationships with the members of those racial groups. During the last phase, one reaches a balanced point. The balance includes collaborative experiences and choices an individual has throughout his or her process of identification. Successfully attaining this process and arriving at this final phase might be explained as a level of comfort achieved within their own racial group as well as the racial group around them. Throughout an individual's lifetime, a person may repeat and revisit different steps and stages of the process and may also reformulate one's racial identity and perceptions. Repeating and reformulating the process may not be a regression but it might involve a greater and more time-consuming process of integrating new information and reevaluation of ideas from a more mature standpoint.

Hamilton's Afrocentric Resistance Model (1994) was introduced by Robinson and Howard, which is based on the the Nguzo Saba value system developed by Karenga and upon Robinson and Ward's Resistance Modality Model (1991). The Nguzo Saba value system is comprised of Kujichagulia (self determination), Nia (purpose), Umoja (unity), Kuumba (creativity), Ujaama (cooperative economics), Imani (faith) and (collective work and responsibility), which are considered to be seven major principles employed for establishing meaning and setting direction in an individual's life. This model, intertwined with the Nguzo Saba value system and principles, contains some aspects of resistance which might be able to promote and initiate psychological health and satisfy interpersonal relationships for Black men between and within different cultures (Nes, Evans, Segerstrom & 2009). Moreover, these could be the guiding goals, objectives and mission for these men all throughout their career and life beyond college.

The Erikson's Identity Development Model (1980) states that identity is self-defined by an individual focusing on enduring personal characteristics (Scott, Dearing, Reynolds, Lindsay, Baird & Hamill, 2008). In case of an established identity, a person is capable of defining his or her characteristics and what has influenced these origins. Complete identity identification involves clarifying one's ethics, standards and morals, along with a commitment to apply it in future. A number of development theorists consider identity development as an individual's way to present it as a bridge from previous experiences to future. According to Bandura's Social Learning Model (1977), social learning theory is focused on learning from observing things in social context (Scott, et al, 2008). It focuses on the idea that people tend to learn from one another, including concepts like imitation, modeling and observational learning. This research describes theories along with an appropriate application and recommendation of theory-to-practice approach in order to help in creating group interactions, which will enhance the degree of attainment and academic success among Black male students. According to Albert Bandura (1982), self-efficacy is a type of self-assessment carried out while evaluating one's competency for successfully executing a specific course of action, which is necessary for reaching the desired outcome. According to Zajacova, Lynch and Espenshade (2005, p. 679) academic, self-efficacy refers to confidence of students in their own abilities for carrying out such a high level of academic tasks, like writing term papers and preparing for exams. Academic level self-efficacy has been depicted in order to predict both persistence at college and college grades (Chemers, Hu, & Garcia, 2001; Mattern & Shaw, 2010; Zajacova, et al., 2005).

Persistence in Higher Education

Student retention and persistence are challenging problems for universities and numerous studies have examined barriers to persistence, as well as methods to improve persistence. The failure of students to complete their higher education coursework is a growing concern among administrators, researchers, students, and parents. The reduction of students on campuses creates financial difficulties for universities, and can negatively impact their accountability to stakeholders (Lau, 2003). Persistence is extremely critical for private and small institutions that depend on student tuition in order to operate effectively. Enrollment numbers drive financial support from the public sector, so continued enrollment numbers are critical for financial viability.

Colleges and universities are making efforts to be able to understand what factors can lead to poor student persistence and what methods can be employed to enhance student retention rates. The world of higher education is very much interested in learning the factors that allow some students to persist on campuses and others to fail. What universities do know regarding student persistence is that there are different predictors for retaining a student based on the student background, institutional landscape, and student 'entering characteristics' (Johnson, 2008).

A college degree is important for economic security later in life; however, it has been found that slightly less than 30% of White adults hold a college degree, as compared to 15% of African American adults (Cross & Slater, 2001). In 2007, Americans with a high school diploma earned approximately $31,000 per year, while those with a bachelor's degree earned an average of $57,000 (United States Census Bureau, 2009).

On average, a college degree has been found to double the average income of African Americans over those that do not have an education higher than a high school diploma (Cross & Slater, 2001). Cross and Slater pointed out that in 2000, the college graduation rate for White students was 59%, and the college graduation rate for African American students was only 37%. Further, the African American rate decreased one percentage point from the previous year. While there are disparities in educational attainment between Black and White persons, other factors such as first-generation status, socioeconomic status, and gender also play a part in the retention of college students (Kreysa, 2006).

High school effects and characteristics have also been examined to determine persistence to graduation. Johnson examined institutional data, high school data, and individual level characteristics from one doctoral/research university to create a model to predict persistence to graduation (2008). Findings indicated students were more likely to persist to the second year of college if they came from higher family incomes, lived on campus during their first semester, and had either grants, work study, or scholarships to finance their education, as opposed to student loans. Additionally, students were less likely to persist to the second year if they were first generation students, came from greater than a 60 mile radius to the institution, and entered the institution from a high school where a higher percentage of students received free lunch (Johnson, 2008). The same findings were determined when examining the probability of graduation within five years from the institution, though findings lacked significance due to small sample size.

Student Services

Student engagement examines the question of how to involve students in activities in such a way that they are able to acquire skills and knowledge. While there has been some discussion over the impact of engagement activities for all types of student subgroups and populations, most research points out that student engagement has a positive effect on students, and particularly positive effects on grades and persistence (Kuh, 2003). Overall, student success in college has been found to depend on students' level of engagement (Pascarella & Terenzini, 2005).

Students can be seen as benefiting from purposeful student engagement measures.

Students from all backgrounds and all levels of academic preparation have been found to be positively impacted by being engaged on their campuses (Kuh, 2009). While much research has been conducted regarding student engagement, there are still areas for further exploration. While it has been found that student participation leads to higher engagement, the particular aspects of participation that make an impact are important for colleges and universities to determine. Additionally, research can be conducted on how institutions can continue to devise methods to engage students to participate in educationally purposeful activities. Further research regarding how to engage online learners, as well as how to use engagement for policy making and accountability will continue to be important areas to explore (Kuh, 2003). However, what is known regarding purposeful student engagement is that students from all backgrounds can be impacted and as a result, increase their odds of obtaining a bachelor's degree (Kuh, 2003).

Just as students benefit from purposeful engagement practices, institutions are also beneficiaries of engagement on their campuses; this benefit includes higher degree completion rates as a result of higher student engagement. Student engagement is important as the current focus on accountability has brought attention to undergraduate student learning and student learning outcomes (Seifert, Drummond, & Pascarella, 2006).

Decock, McCloy, Liu and Hu (2011) conducted a study using two survey administrations and the Washington State Achievers program to determine if a relationship existed between student engagement and persistence. Student persistence was defined as graduating from the institution.

Retention

"Retention is often operationalized as the percentage of first-time, full-time students returning to the same institution for their second year of college" (Mattern & Patterson, 2009, p. 1). Persistence is defined as continuous enrollment from the entry semester through the end of the next academic year (Simmons, Musoba, & Chung, 2005). They both require the return to the second year but persistence takes more of a stand on finishing that second year. Retention is the word to be used in this study, as the program was initiated the summer before freshman year and included the first year of college. Then we asked, "Can this program ensure a return for a second academic year?" Attrition is defined as students who leave their first institution and do not return to their first one or another institution (Ishitani, 2006). These three terms are used frequently in the study of retention at the college level. The majority of the literature agrees with the definitions stated above.

Attrition gets a great deal of attention, as only about half the students who begin college will receive a degree; this statistic is different when looking at the type of institution and the specific racial populations (Masursky, 1997). Approximately 26 percent of first year students do not return for a second year, and only about 49 percent of those who stay will graduate in five years (Noble, Flynn, Lee, & Hilton, 2007). Black students and other students who belong to low-income households and families are observed to be less likely to remain or persist in White institutions than students who belong to middle class/ middle income earning families even if they overcome their academic challenges (Simmons, et al., 2005; Ishitani, 2006; Titus, 2006; Engstrom & Tinto, 2008; Mattern & Patterson, 2009). Considering that these students all reach the college level, what characterizes them which makes them less likely to persist?

High income students most likely come from a family where there has been experience in the college environment. With this experience comes knowledge of what is to be expected in college and how to navigate. This could be termed 'social capital.' Social capital will communicate the trust, social controls, authority and the norms that a particular person should understand and accordingly adopt in order to achieve success (Laura Walter Perna & Titus, 2005, p. 488). Low income students are less likely to have people with this social capital to help them in prepping for and understanding college. Some low-income and African American students do not reach postsecondary education because of their fear of paying the tuition (Laura W. Perna, 2005). Some of these students are wondering if their future jobs will outweigh the potential loan debt. Perhaps this also applies when these students decide to end their education. Of course, there could be other reasons besides economic ones which could cause students to end their academic career.

To better understand retention, one must first understand why students are leaving postsecondary education prematurely. The major reasons found for student departure are: academic difficulty, adjustment to both academic and social life, goals that are unclear or do not contain the attainment of a degree, uncertainty about why they entered college, lack of commitment, lack of integration and community membership, incongruence with the intellectual and social life of the institution, isolation from other members of the institution, cultural, economic and social forces and the lack of social capital (Smart, 2009; Tinto, 2006).

Different types of postsecondary institutions exhibit differences in their numbers for retention. Low retention rates remain at HBCUs today, with the numbers continually getting lower. Within HBCUs the private institutions have a higher graduation rate. As the size of public HBCUs increased the graduation rate decreased. While as the size of the private institutions increases so too does the graduation rate. Private schools graduate more students in four years than public schools. Non HBCUs were also found to have higher degree attainment in private institutions versus public ones (Mattern & Patterson, 2009). When comparing persistence rates among colleges and then among universities, there is less of a difference among the colleges. Perhaps this is the case because of the smaller size in comparison to universities. There is a 56 percent degree attainment in private institutions and 45 percent in public institutions (Ishitani, 2006). It was observed by Ishitani (2006) that students who attend private colleges were 34% less likely to leave or dropout than students who have enrolled in public colleges.

In a study conducted by Vaughn (2007), the need for selected intervention programs addressing the needs of Black male students was stressed. Examples of intervention programs included: Student African American Brotherhood Organization (SAAB), Morgan MILE, Student Pal Program, The Risk-Point Intervention Program, First-year Learning Team (FlighT) Program, Structured Academic Year (STAY) Program, and Model Institutions for Excellence (MIE) Program, West Virginia University two-semester Program.

Student African American Brotherhood Organization (SAAB) Program, according to Vaughn (2007), promotes a spirit of community services and academic excellence among Black men on over 50 campuses nationwide. The Morgan MILE, Morgan State University program provides academic and mentoring support to African America students. The Risk-point Intervention program conducted by the University of Texas at San Antonio provides interventional academic level support to first year and freshmen students at any of the five specific times when academic risks tend to become observable. First year learning team (FlighT) Program conducted by Southeast Missouri State University provides one of the six holistic living and learning experiences related to community for helping Black male students in the social and academic transition to campus life. Glendale Community College program conducts Student Pal

Program identifying main characteristics of students at-risk in the interest of improving the success and retention of minority group students. Model Institute for Excellence (MIE) programs conducted by Bowie State University gives students support and institutional development activities for successfully recruiting and retaining science, mathematics and engineering students.

A series of critical factors examined by Bonner and Bailey (2006) has helped in promoting an environment of academic success for Black college men. These factors included family influences, support, faculty relationships, self-perception and identity development, peer group influences, and institutional environment. The peer group is considered to be an extremely influential and important academic outcome. By understanding subcultures of peer groups in a clearer way, higher education institutions can be better equipped for designing interventions ensuring that Black men are prepared well for pursuing academic growth and mastering coping skills.

It is emphasized by Svanum and Bigatti (2006) that during the past few decades an impressive range of studies have attempted to explain and identify the critical factors for failure and success of students as they tend to pursue higher education. The extent of this effort is not surprising, given the impact that level of education has in a variety of life domains (Pascarella &Terenzini, 2005), and given the difficulties universities have faced in retaining students (Braxton, 2001; Tinto, 1993).

College success has been variously defined with a focus upon either performance outcomes, such as grades for individual courses or semesters; outcomes such as college persistence, often measured over one or two semesters; and less frequently, degree attainment. Many of these studies have been guided by educational or engagement theories of student success (Bean, 1985; Tinto, 1993). These theories have focused upon student involvement in college and propose a distinctly contextual perspective. Success is influenced by the degree to which students become engaged and involved in academic and other activities of college life. These engagement approaches emphasize what individuals do and what institutions do to encourage and support individual student involvement. Therefore, the main point is that if Black college male students are more engaged in college life, they will theoretically be more academically successful. Student involvement as defined by Astin (1984) captures the attention of student behaviors and actions in engagement theories along with the scope of behavior, which helps in reflecting engagement. Student involvement is referred to as the amount of psychological and physical energy that is devoted by a student to his or her academic experiences (p. 297).

Mentoring

Mentoring programs have had outstanding and positive results. Mentors can be assigned or chosen by the student. Heisserer and Parette (2002) indicate that "choosing a mentor for a student is a relatively simple concept" (p. 2). Mentors should be people with whom the students are in daily contact and should understand the challenges students face. Research on mentoring in higher education confirms the importance of mentoring programs in supporting students in their adjustment to college, academic performance, and/or persistence decisions (Fowler & Muckert, 2004; Patitu & Terrell, 1997; Pfleeger & Mertz, 1995; Salinitri, 2005; Santos & Reigadas, 2004). One example of the use of faculty and student interactions comes as a result of formal and "informal faculty-student contact" (ASHE-ERIC, 2003, p.1 03). These connections build trust, support and provide motivation to the student through difficult educational times. Faculty and student interactions can assist students when picking advisors and mentors. Once the mentor/advisor relationship has been established, the mentor/advisor should provide the mentee/advisee with reliable contact information (Shultz, Colton & Colton, 2001).

The significance of mentoring was examined by LaVant, Anderson and Tiggs (1997) in the case of black male students and in regard to success in higher education. Through their study a number of mentoring programs have been presented. Both informal and formal mentoring programs are explained and analyzed in terms of post-secondary efforts in recruiting and retaining. LaVant, Anderson and Tiggs reviewed a limited number of studies on mentoring programs in higher education conducted for retention of African American male students, who had been reported to have a greater level of satisfaction with respect to their college experiences when they are engaged in mentoring relationships. There are a number of mentoring models that have been profiled: The Meyerhoff Program (University of Maryland, Baltimore County); the Black

Man's Think Tank (University of Cincinnati); Project BEAM (Being Excited About Me; West Virginia University); The Bridge (Georgia State University); The Student African American Brotherhood; and The Black Male Initiative (Texas Southern University). Moreover, it was concluded by LaVant, Anderson and Tiggs that mentoring happens to be one of the most effective tools to recruiting, retaining and enhancing the college experiences of Black male students.

Mentoring is described by Sutton (2006) from a developmental and instructional perspective for understanding the positive impact of effective mentoring on Black male college students in a better way. The study examined two different approaches to mentoring. In spite of positive and effective outcomes, Sutton argued that traditionally designed mentoring programs that are significantly instructional might be helpful in encouraging dependence on the mentor and might be considered as a slow progress from the perspective of development. The mentoring relationship also includes cross-race and cross gender challenges. Mentoring programs that are based on developmental perspectives are considered to promote active learning as compared to a passive learning mode. In a developmental model, a mentor can play the role of a guide, a consultant, a gatekeeper and a teacher. These models have implications for programs designed for Black male students.

Sutton has explored the example of the Student African American Brotherhood (SAAB) in great detail. The objective of this program is to encourage development far beyond just one-on-one interaction with mentor. This is achieved in three different ways: 1) Project ACE, collegiate Black males mentoring high school Black males; 2) advisor to student mentoring conducted at collegiate and K-12 levels; and 3) student to student mentoring at the college level. The peer aspect in these mentoring programs significantly plays an important role in personal development growth. The core values of the programs are accountability, intellectual development, self-discipline, and proactive leadership. They also encourage collaboration with the student support services of the institutions. The environmental factors on the campus that have an influence on mentoring programs are further explored, comparing the positive mentoring at PWIs and HBCUs. In an interview carried out by Stanley L. Johnson Jr. (University of California, Los Angeles) presented in Journal of African American Males in Education with Dr. Jawanza Kunjufu (2011), entitled: Leading Educators Series, Dr. Kunjufu alluded to the condition of coaching and mentoring for African American males. He stated that:

"Every African American Male needs to be exposed to a coach in an organized manner versus 'alley ball' and street games. I make this distinction because students who have coaches learn discipline, goals, and have an adult mentor. Street ball does not afford discipline whereas structured sports makes students adhere to them" (p. 143).

Support Network

According to Howard (2010), the early arrival program developed by Ohio State University which focused on Black male achievement has been successful. The center staff provided resources to African American students upon arrival for establishing their willingness to help them possibly all the way through college. These support programs focus on individual achievements, acquisition of leadership skills, positive role modeling and individual needs. As stated by Dr. James, the support center was established in 2004 as the African American center for concern in light of the poor rate of retention of Black male students at Ohio State University. As stated by Harper (2006), it is argued by the Acting White hypothesis of Signithia Fordham and John Ogbu (1986) that African American peer groups' school achievement is usually observed to be acting as "White" to the concept and that of the internalized racism, through which socially stigmatized groups recycle and accept negative messages about their abilities and capabilities. The research revealed that Black men achieving higher grades at six different PWIs relate most of their academic success to the support provided by their peers of the same race. It has explored and examined the significance of peer groups in terms of college experiences of high-achieving Black male students at six PWIs in the Midwest. There was no evidence found in their study about internalized racism in the Black male leadership and academic achievement domain.

According to Patton (2006), students have expressed the importance of Black Culture Centers (BCC) on campuses. The physical presence of the buildings, along with the human aspects, represent recognition of Black culture, people and history, thus providing positive interactions for those who visit the center. These factors provide a context for students to learn about themselves, feel appreciated and supported at PWIs. As campuses grow increasingly diverse, so do the needs of college students. BCCs represent a space that has the potential to address these needs and many more. The benefits of BCCs are reflected in the voices of students who wish to have a safe space within reason. Sources indicate that BCCs contribute greatly to the student experience and make a difference for Black students at PWIs.

Theoretical Framework

Tinto's Model

Dr. Vincent Tinto is known for his extensive research on student retention in the higher educational arena, particularly on the impact of effective learning communities on student enrollment and retention. As stated by Iris (2012), Dr. Vincent Tinto completed his doctoral degree in education and sociology at the University of Chicago.

Dr. Tinto is currently employed at Syracuse University where he serves as a distinguished professor and chair for the higher education program. His passion for student retention has led him to serve as a research consultant for a variety of different national and international organizations.

Tinto's research primarily focuses on the factors that lead to and predict student departure from higher educational institutions. Thus, his 1987 study is one of the theoretical models that guided this research study. In an effort to improve student retention, Tinto (1987) outlined three distinct stages of student development: separation, transition, and incorporation (Isis, 2012). The initial stage, separation, emphasized discarding previous affiliations and acquiring new affiliations at college. The second phase, transition, stresses that individuals become associated with different communities at college (Isis, 2012). The last stage is the incorporation stage that suggests individuals integrate into the community as a whole. Tinto (1987) strongly believed that these stages help with the identification of factors that lead to and predict student development and degree persistence.

Critical Race Theory- Application by Shaun Harper

Dr. Shaun A Harper has received an Emregong Scholar Award in 2005 and Annuit Coepits Award in 2006 for early career achievements. There have been more than 100 research papers, symposia and workshops presented by Dr. Shaun Harper. Most of his work is based on Black men students. In different studies, Shaun Harper has used critical race theory for identifying the attitudes and factors that affect those attitudes among Black students. Though one of his studies conducted on policies that tend to affect the enrollments and rates of degree attainment among Black students, Harper (2009) has used Critical Race Theory as an analytical framework. This framework helped in understanding how racist ideologies and white supremacy have undermined and shaped different policy efforts.

In another of his research works, Harper (2009b) citing Delgado and Stefancic 2001, highlighted that Critical race theorists conceive that White people who try to improve the conditions and status of racial minority groups have been rarely observed doing so without recognizing their own gains and costs associated with making such efforts. Therefore, most of the people benefited from their work on behalf of or with the minority groups. Harper (2009a, 2009b, 2012) has used critical race theory as a framework to critique the meritocracy claims, to provide a voice to Black males experiencing racism, and to illustrate how White educational institutions and personnel would be able to benefit from increasing investments in Black males achievement.

LITERATURE REVIEW GRAPHICAL ILLUSTRATION

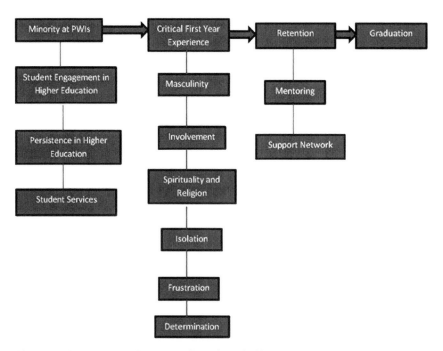

Figure 3: Literature Review Graphical Illustration

Summary

The literature provided evidence that the retention of Black males at predominantly White institutions can be improved. Literature provided studies and research that were focused on different factors related to Black male students' experiences at PWIs. A number of studies have been conducted that focus on different aspects of how Black male students perceive and sustain at PWIs for higher education attainment. However, more research is needed in this area for the retention of first year Black male students at PWIs. Colleges and universities must be vigilant in research endeavors to continue providing literature on the retention of this population. Chapter 3 provided the methodology for this study. The methodology presented: research design; research approach; research strategy; research instrument including interviews; population and sampling; data collection including interviews; data analysis method and role of the researcher.

CHAPTER 3:
METHODOLOGY

The main purpose of this research was to analyze and identify conditions or factors that have been contributing to the retention of the first year Black male students at predominantly White private institutions. The data collected for this research analyzed the case of one White private institution located in the Washington, D.C. area. This chapter provided information about the research strategy, research design, and research approach that was used for conducting the study. Furthermore, the chapter provided information about how data was collected, the sampling method that was used, and how the data was analyzed. Methodology included first meeting with SanMag Cultural Student Services Center African American Male group to secure participants' consent. This was identified by the assistance of the SanMag Cultural Student Services Center associate director. Second, the writer met individually with all six participants: three second semester freshmen and three sophomores and conducted interviews. Third, transcribed data from each participant. Finally, analyzed the data collected from each participant: Data was analyzed to support concepts and themes found within and across narratives.

Research Design

The research employed a qualitative research design for conducting this study. Qualitative research is defined by Creswell (2009) as process for investigating about different factors. This is mainly focused on exploring different factors that are influencing people to behave in a certain manner. With respect to this study, the research explored the impact of pre-college and in-college factors that affect Black male students' experiences and their decisions about whether they want to stay or they want to dropout.

As defined by Creswell (2009), qualitative researchers want to understand and explore the causes or factors that lead toward the occurrence of certain phenomena. It helps in identifying the meanings derived by people about the situations they face (Merriam, 2012, p. 6). Qualitative research is explained as a subjective and scientific approach. It seeks to find answers in a systematic manner using a predefined set of procedures. Qualitative research focuses on sharing characteristics. In addition to this, it seeks to find answers regarding a given topic or problem. Qualitative research was helpful in effectively obtaining information in qualitative form and wording. The qualitative research is capable of providing an in-depth analysis of complex textual descriptions regarding the way people think and experience a particular issue subjected to research. A qualitative research approach helps in analyzing the humanistic approach of an issue that involves contradictory and similar behaviors, opinions, relationships, beliefs, and emotions of people.

The data being collected was very descriptive and authentic and assisted with the search for understanding. A qualitative approach for this study allowed the researcher to understand the participants' perspectives on academic success experiences and how actions, meanings and events, are usually formed and shaped by various situations and circumstances in which they occurred. It is stated by Ragin and Amoroso (2011) that theorists and researchers tend to use a qualitative research method when they believe that in-depth study is the best way of constructing proper representation of a particular phenomenon. Many times researchers address phenomena which, according to them, have been seriously misrepresented. In some cases it is misrepresented by social researchers and authors with help from different approaches, or many times it has not been represented at all. Qualitative research method is generally used by researchers for capturing the voices of the respondents in order to perceive their reality, their singular events, and make sense of the lifestyle in which they are engaged. This method was used for conducting this research.

A qualitative approach allowed the researcher to collect rich data through interviews and to analyze the stories of the participants. From the perspective of the qualitative method, it is far more suitable to understand the experiences of students by the use of words in comparison to quantitative methods. According to Denzin & Lincoln (2011), qualitative research focuses on answering questions related to social or life experiences and thereby, it gives meanings to these experiences. In regard to studies involving college students, qualitative methods such as in-depth interviews, afford participants the freedom to choose aspects of campus life on which to reflect so that it is possible to collect foreseeable, as well as unanticipated information, about their experiences. Whitt, Kuh and Associates (2010) suggest that qualitative studies are appropriate and particularly helpful for student affairs professionals and other people who tend to be interested in developing an understanding about the experiences of undergraduate students.

The researcher believes that in order to identify and understand the experiences of students, it is more appropriate to hear the stories in their own voices as they have actually lived through the situations. The researcher believes that expressions and feelings are more powerful, meaningful, and valid when explained through words rather than statistics and numbers.

Research Approach: Narrative study Approach

Stories have emerged as a popular form of qualitative research, particularly in social science and education. Narration brings researchers and educators together collaboratively to construct school experiences. According to Ollerenshaw (2002), narrative inquiry focuses on highlighting the importance of learning and adopting from participants in a particular setting. This learning usually occurs by listening to stories told by individuals, such as students, and teachers (Clandinin, Pushor & Murray, 2007). The data usually comes from observations in the classroom, interviews, as well as informal conversations with students. Narrative inquiry takes into consideration that people live complex lives. It reflects that people are constantly changing and reports on more than the participants' stories. Storytelling is a reflective act. The process of telling other stories is educative because it goes beyond writing for the self since the story has an audience, as well as an imagined response, and an actual response (Clandinin, Pushor & Murray, 2007). The meaning of the story then becomes reshaped, as well as the meaning of the world to which the story refers. Daiute and Fine (2003) state that the narrative research involves searching for meanings, so the told and the telling, the heard and the written, are inextricably connected and associated as is the narrator as an individual in the social environment of discussion. Narrative inquiry is the best epistemological approach because it scrutinizes how power, culture, and society impact a person's life. This methodology assists with making the invisible - visible.

According to Bell (2010) narrative research depends on the epistemological assumptions by which we as humans can make sense of our experiences with the help of developing individual story structures. This means that we tend to select and recognize those moments from our experiences to which we will attend, and then we frame those chosen elements in a manner that reflects our stories. Narrative inquiry allowed the researcher to analyze experiences holistically in all their complexities and richness. They are powerful constructions, which can function as instruments of social control. Bloom (2002, as cited by Lyle, 2009), explains how carefully interpreted narratives can illuminate how an individual life, different dominant ideologies, and power relations in society are maintained, reproduced, or subverted. Narrative allows marginalized groups to participate in interpreting their experience. The value of narrative is that it allows the researcher to understand the participant's experiences. Life of human beings matter, but much of the research tends to look at the outcomes of the research and ignores the influence of the experiences in their lives. Narrative inquiry illuminates the temporal notion of experience, recognizing that one's understanding of people and events changes (Lyle, 2009).

Storytelling is in the words of Clandinin and Connelly (1994):

"A process of moving simultaneously in four directions: inward (inside self), outward (toward community), backward (in time), and forward (also in time). What one does in telling something to another is to engage in sharing a story, an event or situation that moves in each of these directions. There is also another important aspect of sharing stories from the past in the light of present knowledge. It is not enough to retell the same story in the same way across time if that story is to be used to connect with new meaning and inform us in the present (Clandinin & Connelly, 1994). Rather, a story remembered must be revisited using our own life experience across the intervening years" (Clandinin& Connelly, 1994).

Research Instrument

The instrument of the study included introductory script, interview guide and alternative consent form for research containing human subjects. All are included in the appendices.

INTERVIEWS

The main method of data collection was through in-depth interviewing. The purpose of in-depth interviews is to learn and view the world the way the person being interviewed sees it. According to Creswell (2009):

"The interviews are based on usually open-ended and semi-structured questions which are few in number. They intend to obtain opinions and views of participants regarding a particular phenomena, situation or events" (Creswell, 2009, p. 188).

Leedy and Ormrod (2010) determined that interviews could be flexible and, if conducted correctly, yield interesting information. In analyzing the data to understand how Black males achieve academic success, the holistic content will be the best fit (Ely, 2009). This approach will allow the researcher to determine if sections of the narrative, opening or closing, bring meaning under the light of content which is obtained from the rest of the narrated story or in terms of the entire story. This mode of analysis basically takes into consideration the entire story and focuses on its content.

The researcher submitted a copy of the questions instrument to committee members for review and comments for validity. The instrument was revised based on comments from the committee. Interview questions laid specific emphasis on pre-collegiate and college factors to gain a better understanding for the academic success of first year Black male students at predominantly White private institutions. Literature has found that these questions are necessary to understand the retention of first year Black male students at predominantly White private institutions. Those questions are included in Appendix B.

Population / Sampling

As explained by Creswell (2009) sampling is the selecting of respondents suitable for the research topic. In order to become more familiar with the participants, the research provided a brief biographical summary regarding each participant. In order to protect the identity and location of all the participants, pseudonyms were used. Participants were three second semester freshmen, and three sophomores. The researcher randomly selected three first year second semester Black male students along with three second year Black male students to participate in the study. A nominal incentive in the amount of $25.00 was awarded to each participant. All students selected participated in the research. As stated by Creswell (2009), each individual received an equal opportunity by applying random sampling or random selection technique, making sure that the sample would be good enough to represent the entire population. The researcher obtained the list of three second semester freshmen and three sophomore Black male students that were in good academic standing with a 2.5 GPA and above from the director of the SanMag cultural Student Services Center. Access to the director was in the form of a letter written by my committee Chairlady, Dr. Joan Jackson. This White private institution was chosen because it is located in the Washington, D.C. area.

DATA COLLECTION

INTERVIEWS

The instrument for the study included a cover letter (OR-in-person description). The cover letter (OR-in-person description) included: purpose of the study which is researcher's doctoral dissertation; description of the nature of the study; selection of the participants; provision of assurances to participants that the information that they provided would be kept confidential. Interviews were conducted individually for each participant. Scheduled interviews lasted approximately 60-90 minutes for each participant.

After the approval of IRB from both Argosy and this White private institution, all of the interviews were held at the SanMag Cultural Student Services Center at this predominantly White private institution. The researcher collected data from each participant based on pre-collegiate and collegiate experiences. All interviews were audio taped and transcribed verbatim. The researcher preserved the essence of the spoken word so that grammar or any language structure were not corrected. Questions used during the interview process were open-ended such as: "Tell me about your freshman experience. What were your first impressions of this institution?" Possible emerging themes might include: positive interactions with high school teachers and/or guidance, recognition of academic success, student involvement, reading and studying, enhancing development skills, forming study groups, learning time management skills, discipline, and overall balance.

Data Analysis Method

This section discussed the procedures to implement in the analysis of data that was collected. Analysis of data is an ongoing and recursive process that is concurrent with data collection. According to Lincoln and Guba (1985), data analysis may be defined in its simplest terms as the process of "making sense" of the data. The following procedures for data analysis were utilized in order to "make sense" of the qualitative portion of the data that was collected.

1. *Transcription* – Data was transcribed within a week of the recorded interview. The data from the interviews were organized according to the research questions of the study and review for categories, themes, and patterns (Creswell, 1998). Transcripts from narratives were read and reread, as well as notes which were taken while listening to the recorded interviews, field journal remarks on how the researcher was impacted, and comments from observations. The researcher proceeded to learn to think in idiosyncratic language and the meaning-system of the participant (Josselson, 2004, p.9) to understand their frame of reference and assumptive world.
2. *Thematic and Semi-Structural analysis* – Data analysis followed the strategies described by Riessman (2008). Thematic and semi-structural analysis were utilized to interpret the data collected from the participant interviews. Analysis interprets and compares biographies as they are constituted in the research interview (Riessman, 2008). According to Riessman (2008), thematic analysis allows the investigator to work with a single interview at a time, isolating and ordering relevant episodes into a chronological biographical account. After the process had been completed for all interviews, the researcher zoomed in, identified the underlying assumptions in each account and named (coded) them.

3. *Holistic/Content Analysis* – Lieblich, Tuval-Mashiach, and Zilber (1998) offer a model that will assist with the analysis and organization of narrative. The holistic approach takes into account the life experiences and stories of a person as a whole. The parts of the text will be interpreted in the context of different parts of the narrated stories. Content focuses on what happened, why it happened, who participated in the event, all from the standpoint of the storyteller.

In analyzing the data to understand the way Black males achieve academic success, the holistic content was the best fit. This approach allowed the researcher to determine if sections of the narrative, the opening or closing, bring meaning under the light of material that emerges from the other narrated parts or in terms of the narrated story on the whole. This mode of analysis basically takes into consideration the entire story and focuses on its content.

Although it is important to focus on themes and semi-structures articulated by the participants, the researcher also scrutinized nonverbal communication and meanings that are less conscious (interpersonal space, body movement, posture, volume, and pitch (Fontana & Frey, 2008).

In light of the various recommendations mentioned in the review of literature section, the researcher focused themes related to the academic success of Black male students at predominantly white private institutions. Throughout the process the researcher engaged with the literature, and where new themes emerged, the researcher sought after relevant research.

Finally, the researcher presented the results by using vignettes from the interviews to support concepts and themes found within and across narratives. Geertz (1973) refers to presenting narrative results as a continuous dialect between the most local and global details in such a manner that both can be viewed and examined simultaneously (p. 239). Reporting was organized by participant and in chronological order, starting with the first scheduled interview. Numbers of similar responses from the participants were recorded as the quantitative aspect of this study.

Role of the Researcher

My role as a researcher was 'participant observer' and offered semi-structured interviews with my participants. The researcher is a Black male who has attended a predominantly White private institution. The researcher experience was explained to the participants in order to enable them to identify with him. As a researcher, I sought advice from my dissertation committee to ascertain that I was conducting a proper qualitative research. The researcher bias to this study is that he did attend predominantly White private institutions and applied some of the literature principles to achieve academic success. The researcher is a Black male who went to the institution to obtain his Master's degree in Software Systems. To mitigate this bias, the researcher encouraged other Black male students who want to attend predominantly White private institutions that they can be academically successful by following the literature provided in this study. Most especially, Black males must have the desire to succeed. The researcher mitigated personal bias by allowing other Black male students to share their experiences and analyzed their experiences on the basis of their narrated stories. In order to keep the research from being influenced by personal bias, the researcher recorded the notes and then read them and reread them in order to keep personal thoughts and opinions from influencing the analytic aspects.

Conclusion

This chapter illustrated the procedures that were used in this study, the rationale for qualitative research, the utilization of narrative inquiry and the research instrument. The researcher identified the actions to be taken to ensure proper procedures for data collection, the process that was used to address confidentiality and ethical protection of the participants, and the method for analysis as they were implemented. Chapter four deals with the analysis and results of the data.

CHAPTER 4:
DATA ANALYSIS AND RESULTS

This is a phenomenological study that provided relevant information to conditions or factors that contributed to the retention of first year Black male students at predominantly white private institutions. Research data looked at such an institution of higher learning as located in the Washington, D.C. area. The topic is important because it provided evidence from the data collected to high school Black male senior students who may desire to attend predominantly white private institutions (PWPI). The problem area in the study were the academic accomplishments of first year Black male students at predominantly White private institutions (PWPI), specifically their experiences and the key factors that contributed to their academic success. The study used such a university's definition of students being in good academic standing (2.5) grade point average and above in determining academic success. Problems that were studied are academic performance, unwelcome environments, background of first year Black male students, spirituality, the inclusion of Black Male Students into various campus activities and the acceptance of them into the social life on campus.

This study was guided by the central research question: **What conditions or factors contribute to the retention of first year Black male students at predominantly White private institutions?** In order to gain an understanding of academic success, it was important to have sub-questions related to campus involvement, social life, and cultural identity that may contribute to retention. As mentioned, this study used a qualitative research design. According to Creswell (2009), qualitative inquiry involves systematic collection, organization, and interpretation of material derived from speech and observation.

Research Setting

The SanMag Cultural Student Services Center (SCSSC) at this private institution stands firmly in its role as an institution center for cultural communication, community building, and leadership. The center collaborates with major university offices including: the office of the vice provost for diversity and inclusion, the center for student engagement, the community service, graduate admissions, and the counseling center. In partnership with these allies the center strives to develop co-curricular and experiential learning opportunities for this institution's students that: 1) Support the shaping of a campus climate that welcomes cultural, racial, ethnic, and intellectual diversity 2) Support the academic, cultural, social, spiritual and professional growth of the students it serves and 3) Support the retention, inclusion and increase in participation rates of students of color. One of the main initiatives that is effective and was implemented is the Black Men Initiative (BMI). This initiative focuses solely on the retention and timely graduation of African-American males.

The matriculation rate of African American students for 2013 was 7.21%. From this percentage, 3.2 % were Black male and 4.01% were Black female students. This predominantly White private institution first year retention rate for all students is 94%. First year Black male students retention rate is 84.9% due to the apportionment of 3.2% matriculation. This institution has provided numerous forms of assistance to aid in the retention of first year Black male students. Assistance provided academic support services that were available to Black male students including, but not limited to, weekly late night study hours, mentoring and strategic partnerships with academic offices, and outside organizations such as the Institute for Responsible Citizenship and INROADS. This predominantly White private institution is committed to the holistic growth and development of first year Black male students to ensure that their experiences at this institution is one that promotes the benefits of relationship building and access to relevant resources.

Background on Participants

Participant 1

Participant 1 is a native of Washington, D.C. He attended a local private high school in the Washington, D.C. area. He is currently a sophomore majoring in Communication. He is currently serving as the assistant editor in chief of the A's magazine which is the publication of the Black Student Union. He is from a single family household and he is a first generation college student. His grade point average is 2.9.

Participant 2

Participant 2 was born in Washington, D.C. to Nigerian parents. He attended a local private high school in the Washington, D.C. area. He is currently a sophomore majoring in Biology. He wants to become a medical doctor to help find the cure for malaria in Africa and other places in the world. He likes body building and would like to have his own body building business besides his medical career. His parents are well educated and have been contributing to the community for over twenty years. His grade point average is 3.0.

Participant 3

Participant 3 was born in the 8th ward of Washington, D.C. He attended public high school in Washington, D.C. He is a second semester freshman and is majoring in Business/Finance. His birth parents are still married and have various university degrees. He is the only child of his parents. He is involved with organizations that help to research and prevent AIDS. His grade point average is 2.8.

Participant 4

Participant 4 was born in North Carolina. He relocated with his father to the Washington, D.C. area after his parents' divorce. He attended a private high school in Prince George County, Maryland. He is a sophomore majoring in Psychology. He is a member of

ABPsy, a psychology organization on campus. His grade point average is 3.7.

Participant 5

Participant 5 was born in Washington, D.C. to a single mother. He attended a private high school in Washington, D.C. He is an only child. He is currently a second semester freshman. He is majoring in Accounting. He is a first generation college student. He wants his mother and grandmother to be proud of him when he graduates from college. His grade point average is 3.5.

Participant 6

Participant 6 was born in the Washington, D.C. area. His father was killed when he was ten years old. His mother has never remarried since the death of his father. He is closest to his mother and grandmother. He is a second semester freshman majoring in political science. He started a student organization calls DMV club to serve D.C., Maryland and Virginia. The primary objective of this club is to encourage young black males to come together and share their unique experiences. His grade point average is 2.6.

Table 2: Background Information of Participants

Participants	Type of High School	Year in college	Major	1st Generation	Parents: Status	College Grade Point Average
1	Private	Sophomore	Communications	Yes	Single	2.9
2	Private	Sophomore	Biology	No	Married	2.9
3	Public	Freshman	Business - Finance	No	Married	2.8
4	Private	Sophomore	Psychology	No	Divorced	3.7
5	Private	Freshman	Accounting	Yes	Single	3.5
6	Private	Freshman	Political Science	Yes	Widow	2.6

Table 2 provides a clear explanation on all six participants. Five of the participants graduated from private high schools, one graduated from public high school, three are sophomores and three are second semester freshmen, all six have various majors, two parents are married, two parents are single, one parent is divorced and one parent is a widow. Grade point averages range from 2.6 to 3.7. All are currently from the Washington, D.C. area.

Data Collection

Data collection was done by face to face interviews of six Black male students at the SanMag Cultural Student Services Center at one predominantly White private institution in the Washington, D.C. area. Three second semester first year and three sophomores Black male students were interviewed to learn of their academic success at this private institution. Interview questions dealt with pre-collegiate and collegiate factors to determine the readiness and determination to be academically successful in completing their college education. Kindly see appendix B for interview protocol questions dealing with participants' pre-collegiate and collegiate factors.

Emerging Themes

The researcher identified eleven emerging themes from the participants' pre-collegiate and collegiate factors. These factors appeared to help the participants to achieve academic success at this predominantly White private institution in the Washington, D.C. area. The eleven major findings were from pre-collegiate and collegiate experiences of the participants in achieving academic success. The major pre-collegiate findings were: a) positive interactions with high school teachers or guidance and mentors' assistance for college preparation, band and b) parents and family members' encouragement and support to attend college. Major collegiate findings were a) involvement with retention programs on campus, b) social life on campus toward Black male students, c) participation in leadership roles on campus, d) participation with mentoring programs on campus, e) student involvement, f) religion and spirituality, g) dealing with and overcoming frustration, h) determination to complete college and i) the importance of social network on campus and the benefits for attending this predominantly White private institution. These themes are directly related to the literature review presented in Chapter 2.

The participants are a minority at this particular institution; they are engaged in higher education; three of them are experiencing the critical first year experience and three of them have already experienced the critical first year; all of them are black male students dealing with their various masculinity issues; they are all involved in activities on campus to keep them abreast of all opportunities; they are all spiritually grounded; they all experience isolation and find means to deal with isolation; they are all frustrated with some conditions on campus; they are all determined to complete their college education; they are all persistent in getting all of their assignments completed to move to the next level in their disciplines; they are involved in student services by helping with security and newcomer orientation; they are all involved with what the SanMag

Cultural Student Services Center retention program calls Black Men Initiatives where they are paired up with upperclassmen who provide them advice on retention and its importance to achieve academic success; they are all involved in the mentoring programs provided by the SanMag Cultural Student Services Center and furthermore, they are appreciative of the social network on campus.

Pre-Collegiate Factors

Research Question: *What conditions or factors contribute to the retention of first year Black male students at predominantly White private institutions?*

Theme 1: Positive Interactions with High School Teachers or Guidance and Mentors' Assistance for College Preparation

Five of the participants expressed their appreciation and the support received from teachers for college readiness. Positive teacher-student relationships is evidenced by teachers' reports of low conflict, a high degree of closeness and support, and little dependency — have been shown to support students' adjustment to school, contribute to their social skills, promote academic performance, and foster students' resiliency in academic performance (Battistich, Schaps, & Wilson, 2004). Participant 1 expressed his experience by saying:

> "Ah….he was my junior year English teacher. So he was my first teacher for AP exams so he really prepared me for college level courses."

Participant 3 expressed:
> "Hum.. I guess in a way she taught me how that I can't depend on the teacher all the time to do anything. Sometimes you have to go out there on your own to find things because some teachers you know, as great they can be, they don't offer like everything to you so you have to find your own stuff."

Participant 4 expressed:
> "Ah.. I don't know. She was inspiring and ah…she just you know, the warm way which I was treated and ah…

the support she gave in class talking about life as well as being a good teacher and student relationship and ah…you know, it just overall helped me to be comfortable at the school. As I said, you know, I moved up here end of my 10th grade year and I ah…didn't know a lot of people ah.. I didn't have deep relationship like the other students. Ah..that didn't matter with her. She was a very good lady. If I needed to sit and talk, she was there for me."

Participant 5 expressed:

"She ah….she kinda taght me like not to give out. Persistence…ah, just to make sure that when I did move to college that I sought my teachers for exact help when I need it. And ah…just to take more initiative and making sure that I get the best education."

Participant 6 expressed:

"Ah…..she…I think she allowed all of us in our class including myself to ah..to kind of reassess where we were ah..as students because we were in her honor, ah.. you know she taught honors classes and advance placement courses so most of the students in our class you know were at the top of our class and so we felt like we were where we needed to be ah..in terms of academic rigor ah…but I think that she challenged us ah..and ah..I think that even though she challenged us she, she also supported us ah..because you know there are folks who will challenge you and let you fail ah…..then start to start all over but you know in high school, there isn't no starting over unless you, you know go stay back but ah..she challenged us but also gave us the support that we needed to get through the work. Ah….I thought that

> was very good and I will say that's how she contributed to my success in high school."

Five participants in the study indicated that dealing with teachers or guidance helped them tremendously for college readiness. By interacting with teachers on a daily basis to understand subjects being taught for college level courses made them to realize the rigor that lay ahead after high school.

All of the participants expressed their appreciation for having mentors or counselors. Mentoring programs have had outstanding and positive results. Mentors can be assigned or chosen by the student. Heisserer and Parette (2002) indicate that "choosing a mentor for a student is a relatively simple concept" (p. 2). Mentors should be people with whom the students are in daily contact and understand the challenges students face.

Participant 1 expressed:
> "Yes."

Participant 2 expressed:
> "Yes, most definitely. When it came to ah..even deciding schools because back when I was finishing my junior year in high school, I had decided to apply to eight schools. Then my counselor said that I should try this program called IMPACT. It is a college preparatory problem here in DC. Ah.. so with that, they paired us up with another mentor and with this individual they really emphasize that we should explore our options. We shouldn't limit ourselves to eight or ten schools. So I ended up applying to twenty five schools for college and just being able to have those options to choose from, I believe that was a very high point in that transition

DATA ANALYSIS AND RESULTS 123

between high school and college because we were looking at those many schools we were going to apply and I don't think most students are exploring their deep horizon—[they are] limiting themselves."

Participant 3 expressed:

"We had one and he was very active in like doing our academic planning of courses to the end of high school to college but I used him more like a resource."

Participant 4 expressed:

"Ah.. I did actually—I had a really good counselor at Wise by the name of Mr. Byrd and I would go and sit with him and we talked about, you know, preparing for SAT, ACT talk about colleges and applications. He was another inspiring individual too you know. I think he and Mrs. Dobbins saw something in me and you know, they sort of helped me to feel appreciated and special not that I [was] any better or different than the other kids; but you know, they saw a talent in me and the desire to learn and to success ah..in my endeavors and stuff that I think that's what caused them to help me out in whatever [way] they could."

Participant 5 expressed:

"I spoke a lot with my scholarship adviser on a lot of college courses and things like that so she was the person I talked to a lot. She was very helpful in helping me narrowing down my choices ah… and to try to get the most financial aid out of the school that I looked at."

Participant 6 expressed:

"Ah.. yes. We had ah.. we actually had a college counselor at my high school that was very helpful ah.. that wasn't helping in high school but also wanted for us to go to college ah… I will say I used him very frequently ah.. as a resource ah..to you know wanted to get advice about you know what I should do to get from point A to point B in high school but also what I needed to ah.. [achieve] from the start of high school to the finish to best prepare myself for college ah.. and so that's the way I utilized my counselor in high school."

Mentor assistance for these participants in the study for college preparation was beneficial to them. They expressed assistance and appreciation for the assistance given to them by their mentors and counselors. They finally realized that it takes a lot of preparation to enroll in college.

Theme 2: Parents and Family members' Encouragement and Support to Attend College.

All the participants in the study indicated that their parents and family members definitely encouraged them to attend college. Their parent and family members' encouragement stems from the fact that a college education especially for Black males is very important if they wish to survive in today's job market—for them to be successful in supporting their families and communities.

Participant 1 expressed with excitement:
"Yes."

Participant 2 expressed:
> "Yes sir. Hum….I didn't have any choice" (laughter).

Participant 3 expressed:
> "Yes, definitely."

Participant 4 expressed:
> "They did. Ah..I can say there were no other options. Both of my parents graduated with bachelor's degrees from Bethel State University in North Carolina. They both attended HBCU but ah.. they really saw the importance and the significance of college education or college degrees and I saw them struggling even with their college degrees, and I did [not] want to work at Albees for the rest of [my] life."

Participant 5 expressed:
> "Yes….ah I come from a single parent household so it was me, my mother, my grandmother. Ah..my mother and my grandmother they really encouraged me to go to college. Ah… Nobody in my family have ever gone to college. So this was a first for the family as a whole sending me to school as the first, ah..so I had the support of my mother, my grandmother and my family and all the rest of my community because you know it is very rare in my community for people to go to college and I was one of them who did, so I had a lot of support to come to college."

Participant 6 expressed:
> " Oh man, I mean, ah …yes, yes and yes."

For family members' encouragement;
Participant 1 expressed:
> "Ah..yes everyone was pretty encouraging and supportive for me to attend college."

Participant 2 expressed:

> "Oh yes. Most definitely, especially everybody in the community is just happy for me and just making sure to encourage me by saying that it is the first step. I guess you must have other goals, work towards them and realize every day to get closer to your success. My mother always says it will come a time in this country that you will need a PhD to obtain a job" (laughter).

Participant 3 expressed:

> "Yes, I do..I am the only child. Both of parents are very supportive. They are very proud of me. I tried and that kind of it is almost like a driving force to do well. It is not like public school where you are basically for yourself so yes even though it is not so, yes. You know, here it is out of pocket even with scholarships and so you know their investment is on the line so I have to do well and have to make sure that, you know, whatever they put in they see something good comes out. They are always supportive they are proud of me and I do try as much as I can."

Participant 4 expressed:

> "Yes sir. Ah,… I do. Ah..my dad is a good source of support. I do work. Ah…I work two jobs and so I actually provide mostly for myself. My dad works here and because of that I don't have a large amount of tuition. We have to pay only 11%. But he actually pays that for me. He is doing that so when I graduate with my bachelor's degree I would not have a large debt. He usually put money in my account to help me out on various occasions. I get moral support for my mother and grandmother."

Participant 5 expressed:
> "Yes. I do, yes. It kind of ah....yes, they are still in my corner."

Participant 6 expressed:
> "Ah.. I am an only child. It was very important to my mom ah..just because I am her only child so that was very important for her. But my entire family is very supportive by asking what I am doing if I need anything you know and so it is good to have that support system at home to make sure that whatever I need, you know, studying is one thing but making sure you know, if I need food, (laughter) if I need clothes and just making sure that I have that stuff that supports me in my goals, my family is very supportive of that too."

Parents and family members play an important role in motivating their children to attend college. The constant reminder that you must go to college after high school is prevalent in every African American household. Some Black men struggle tremendously in high school. Therefore the desire to attend college is low. However, when they are placed in a college preparatory environment with assistance from high school administrators and counselors, they tend to enroll in college and become academically successful. For this study, the participants are all enrolled in a predominantly White private university and all of them live in the Washington, D.C. area. All have graduated from high schools in the Washington, D.C. area.

COLLEGIATE FACTORS

Research Question: *What conditions or factors contribute to the retention of first year Black male students at predominantly White private institutions?*

Theme 3: Involvement with Retention Programs on Campus

In a study conducted by Vaughn (2007), the need for selected intervention programs addressing the needs of Black male students was stressed. In this study the retention program at this predominantly White private institution is the Black Men Initiative (BMI).

Participant 2 expressed:
> "Ah..nothing like on the line of academic probation but more of like bolstering on where I am at academically and helping me to continue to stay on top of my goals and make sure I am involved in a couple of things organization wise. In my freshman year I was involved in the boys gospel choir and that was just another good thing for the part everybody has around the same belief, same goals and things of that nature. Ah….academically, there have been a couple of organizations that I have been working with and also black men initiative here on campus which is a good program in which they separate us with upperclassmen to help us with anything we need help with like our specific areas of study or just need someone to talk about in that nature. I know there have been a couple of times when we come here and have our BMI (Black Men Initiative) meetings and afterward there is someone around that we report to and making sure we are happy and making sure who we are and what we about and making sure we are striving towards our goals."

Participant 3 expressed:
> "Oh yes....Oh yes. Ah...for starters, first semester, I joined the newspapers and that's been very exciting because ah...I have not done too much second semester but first semester ah..one of the cool things that I did was I went to cover the Democratic National Watch Party and so I got to interview ah...bunch of D.C. council members and Vincent Gray too, so that was good. I am also in the fraternity."

Participant 4 expressed:
> "Ah..not heavily,. There is BMI (Black Men Initiative); I am a member but not being very active. I do frequent this center and talk with the director and assistance director. They let me come in here and print and you know get all the documents I need to use the computer. They are a great help."

Participant 5 expressed:
> "Well.... I think, ah...I am involved with the black men initiative ah..yes...so yes."

Participant 6 expressed:
> "Ah....I am a member of the Black Men Initiative which is ah...one of its goals is Black male retention on campus ah..so having that support system of ah..you know, Black men on campus you know there aren't many of us here at this school but having that support system is very good ah....and I will say other than that I don't think any other will be a retention program but with my scholarship program ah.. I am a Strathanburg scholar here so my scholarship program is really about bringing us all together on campus as a scholar but also supporting us

so that we can, you know, make it through the rigor of college, so I will say those two programs are really you know, the retention programs I am involved in."

Five of the participants in the study stressed the importance of the retention program at this university for having the SanMag Cultural Students Services Center and the Black Men Initiative retention program. They are reinforced by the accomplishments of other Black men when seminars are conducted to stress the importance of getting a college degree. They also expressed their satisfaction for having a place on campus they can visit to appreciate their ethnicity.

Theme 4: Social Life on Campus towards Black Male Students

All of the participants expressed favorable social life on campus towards Black men.

Participant 1 stated:
> "As far as I have seen ah.. everyone gets along. I think we all understand that a place like this ah…where [there aren't] a lot of us so it's kind of necessary to stick together but you know it is better to associate, then to be friendly, than not to be. You know, you sort of realize that we have to stick together because there are not a lot of us and it is important that we all graduate, you know. It is important that we all make it so ah..so I find, you know, that social life with black guys here is pretty good."

Participant 2 stated:

> "It is fine… ah…. We have lots of events..ah… it is okay, actually towards the end of my previous semester ah.. the graduate students actually enable us to, the black student graduate association, ah.. they had their first introductory event towards the end of graduate black society and I think that was a great event just to network and get to know other individuals who have already graduated and are on the next level of their education and I enjoyed that event. More of these events happen during the school year to boost the notion that after you have graduated, there are more you can do and that they have done it and there is nothing we cannot do as well."

Participant 3 stated:

> "Ah..it is so many things to say. I guess it is good in a way that this school is very inclusive to a lot of people that there no sort of like ah..if you go to ah..the Black house party, you will have ah..I will just say it is a little bit separate because they have Black parties and then a white but I could say white but fraternities parties sororities parties that are mostly white individuals and so ah..I wouldn't say it is bad because everybody has something to do. Nobody is left out or something. You have the ability to join either but I feel that in a way it is not as diverse as in terms of everybody interacting with each other is one thing I have noticed."

Participant 4 stated:

> "Ah.. hummm..it is…everything opened. Ah…I am welcome to everything on campus. I am not restricted from anything because I am black. There are white fraternities and sororities and black fraternities and sororities

but every now and then I see some blacks in a white fraternity and what not ah..I say okay, cool. There is some inclusion but not because of one, everyone is like that. I think this school does a good job of ah..being diverse and caters to minorities on campus. They do a very good decent job."

Participant 5 stated:

"Ah…uh…my experience is that the only place you can find social life here is at the SanMag Cultural Students Services Center. This is the only place I am really invited to be. However, a few of the Caucasians are not receptive to Black men or to me on campus. They do not want to be involved with you on class projects. They are all cooped up with other Caucasians. You are only involved with black students. So…ah..yes it is difficult definitely being a Black male on campus. The only place to talk and feel like you're being accepted is at the SanMaag Cultural Student Services Center. So this is like a life saver. Ah…yes."

Participant 6 stated:

"Ah... it is a very small and close-knit community in terms of black male students. Ah….we think we all have a community here ah.. I feel like for the most part we all know each other ah.. and I think organizations like the Black Student Union and Black Men Initiative and just kind of the program here at the MSSC is very important too ah…just because it brings us together ah.. I feel like we all come from different parts of the city but we all come from very similar experiences. Ah.. and so it is good to have that close-knit community. I guess from the outside looking in ah.. you know

I feel like ah… black males on this campus, again it is very few of us here ah..and so ah.. I think it is always good to see, you know, black males blossom socially outside of this kind of circle we have here ah.. for me, ah..I think ah… I feel like my social experience with Black males and just you know, multicultural students here is pretty much my core ah..and then you know, everything else is great but I feel as though the support system and the true friendship that I have so far here really comes from the multicultural community and the relationships I have with black males and other multicultural students on campus. However, the relationship between black and white students is not as organic as the way it should be. So I think that could improve."

They are very grateful for the SanMag Cultural Student Services Center. Since as they put it "we are not many here, therefore we have to stick together" As stated by Tinto (2006) in his model of student retention, social acceptance is very important for retention. When students are accepted socially among their peers, they tend to stay and become academically successful.

Theme 5: Participation in Leadership Roles on Campus

As stated by Harper, S (2007) "previous studies have documented the beneficial effects of engagement in student organizations and out-of-class activities on identity development, retention, and other outcomes produced in college for African American students (p.13).

Participant 1 stated:
> "Yes. I am the assistant editor in chief of the A's magazine which is the publication of the Black Student Union. Ah..I am...I think that's the main one."

Participant 2 stated:
> "Yes...ah.. in one of my organizations, phi beta fraternity I was the treasurer this previous year. Ah..my freshman year, in BMI I was the freshman representative of my class. So every now and then I am looking to different things I can be part of---how to continue to make my study here in college memorable. Also this past year I got a mentee freshman who is also a pre-med as I am and we study together and I help him as much as I can."

Participant 4 stated:
> "Ah. Not sure much. Leadership…..but there are ah… organizations that I am involved in ah… I was a member of a voice a cappella group, gospel choir group for a year during my freshman year. I am a member of ABPsy Association of Black Psychology. I am a psychology major and, you know, I am in charge of their external relationships, for a better word 'advertisement' and I participate in their events and help them set up and I enjoy lot of their exposure."

Participant 6 stated:
> "Ah.. I just finished a term as student association senator. I was one of the six representatives representing the Columbian College ah.. in the senate and ah I started

my own student organization here ah.. the DMV club, the D.C., Maryland and Virginia for local club students for students who grew up or live in the region ah.. just to bring us together ah.. and, you know, just share our experiences—our unique cultural ah.. cultural and social experiences with this university community at large. So those are some of the leadership roles I am involved with on campus."

Participating in leadership roles on campus and being effective in those roles will help to make Black Male students at predominantly White private institutions visible, thereby gaining respect among their peers. Four out of six participants in the study are engaged or were engaged in leadership roles on campus. All of them seem to enjoy the responsibilities they inherited and performed their tasks to the best of their abilities. These roles allowed them to meet other students around campus and interact with them to accomplish a designated task. Their visibility was appreciated by other racial groups on campus.

Theme 6: Participation with Mentoring Programs on Campus

Mentoring is described by Sutton (2006) from a developmental and an instructional perspective for understanding the positive impact of effective mentoring on Black male college students in a better way. The study examined two different approaches to mentoring. In spite of positive and effective outcomes, Sutton argued that traditionally designed mentoring programs that are significantly instructional might be helpful in encouraging dependence on the mentor and might be considered as a slow progress from the perspective of development. The mentoring relationship also includes cross-race and cross gender challenges. Mentoring programs that are based on developmental perspectives are considered to promote active learning as compared to a passive learning mode. In a developmental model, a mentor can play the role of a guide, a consultant, a gatekeeper and a teacher. These models have implications for programs designed for Black male students.

Participant 2 stated:

> "Okay. There is a special mentorship program here which is the BMI (Black Men Initiative). I personally picked up a mentee on my own. So I didn't go through any of the official mentoring programs at this university or BMI to pick up my mentee. It was more like we kind of met and started talking and I let him know that if there are times he needed any help and then after a month at the school we asked to become mentor and mentee. We have similar goals so it is easy to be connected. He is from the Sudan."

Participant 3 stated:

> "Ah.. It was in the sense of during the first semester with Black Men Initiative which is the organization that does mentoring and mine was Austin Boster. Ah.. we contacted a little bit on Facebook but we didn't get together because of time issues. Yes, I guess that will be my mentoring experience."

Participant 6 stated:

> "Ah…I am not particularly involved in any established mentoring programs on campus. But I think that again

from kind of the experience we have at the MSSC I feel like we naturally gain mentors, you know, from the staff members here ah.. you know, from older students here. I feel like we create great and lasting relationships ah.. and I feel like those mentorships are very important to me."

Although only three participants in this study are participating in the mentoring program, they have benefitted a lot from the program and are willing to become mentors to incoming freshmen.

Theme 7: Student Involvement

It is stated by Harper (2006), involvement is considered to be one of the key aspects for the success of Black male students at the collegial level. His study examines the gains (benefits) and outcomes (results) that are connected with outside class activities, especially experiences related to leadership.

Participant 1 stated:
>"Ah..I attend heavily the black student union activities. I release the magazine that I write and edit for about every month or so. I am a member of the ministry club which was designed to help men talk about and prevent sexual assaults in abusing women."

Participant 2 stated:
>"One of the things I like to devote my time to is music. Ah..I have been doing it ever since I was in the middle school. I started with my church ah…I do mentoring with the acolytes, ah..and through high school and just

doing that and being able to give back to the community. There are a lot of people that helped me to get here and to be able to give back is a good feeling."

Participant 3 stated:
"My involvement. Ah…there are a lot of things I have done this past year, one of them will be ah…I participated in this Aids activism ah… I participated in film. My professor in first semester in this class where I really enjoyed was the director of this film. He was organizing a bunch of films that have to do with HIV AIDS and so I was involved in that in a while. Ah…I don't know if you know Tommy Fisher, he wrote this Lincoln screen play and ah…he wrote this play in the early nineties calls Angels in America, so he came over and ah..I think it was April or May and so I was involved in that."

Participant 4 stated:
"Ah..so yes so yes. I am member of ABPsy, ah..I was a member of the voice. I work two jobs. So I work for the university events as one of their student staff. Ah…you know, I help them plan for events that the university is having—commencement being our biggest one and also different dinners and workshops they might host. Ah..I also work for campus security as a student in the student dorm, making sure guests sign the guest list and so forth. So I get to meet a lot of students."

Participant 5 stated:
"Ah…my only involvement is actually with the multicultural group ah..yes. That's basically it. With the SanMag cultural group because all of my life I have always be

around all kinds of people. Their always being white, Hispanics, black all kinds of people. Being here is just like all Whites and a few minorities sitting in the corner ah...so I kind of just gravitate. I am not used to just like just being immersed into so much just one thing that I just don't ah..... I don't feel comfortable being involved with the predominantly White organizations because it doesn't feel like that's mine... I don't feel comfortable. So I try to get involved with the SanMag cultural organization and things like that so...yes."

Participant 6 stated:

"Ah.. you know again I was in the student association so that took me, you know, to very different activities on campus. When I was running for the student association I was at a lot of student organization meetings, lots of campus events ah....but even after, I tried to stay as involved as I could ah...with different pieces of the community. Ah.. but I try to be as active as I can on campus just I like you know, having new experiences on campus and meeting new people ah..and so you know if there is an event that I am interested in, I will try to go to it ah.. and the.. I think, I am not as active as a lot of, you know, students that I see on campus. I feel like students at this school are very active around campus but I think I am still adjusting to the balance between study and campus life but I think I am pretty involved."

All of the participants in the study are involved into different activities on campus. This has enabled them to have access to various organizations, with faculty members, deans and administrators that are heading or monitoring the activities. Given the opportunity to participate and be involved in those activities enhance their social acceptance, thereby giving them a sense of belonging and increasing retention.

Theme 8: Religion and Spirituality

According to research conducted by Watson (2006), religion and spirituality in the lives of Black men in college are topics which are rarely covered by authors and researchers. In his research, Watson (2006) has presented practical definitions of both religion and spirituality. According to his definitions, spirituality is a belief in some animating, external force and Religion is adhering to an established system of practices and beliefs grounded under spirituality. Both religion and spirituality have been playing a significant part in the way African American male college students perceive their responsibilities. Watson identified and analyzed the role played by spirituality in African American male students' lives and how it can be used for developing their identity and helping them to develop their coping skills throughout their college experience. Watson reviewed several perspectives related to spirituality, considering them under a framework of daily practices for Black people. Watson's study was conducted consisting of 97 first year and second year Black male college-going students. The information was obtained about the students' religious and spiritual beliefs and their educational/academic experiences. It was revealed through the findings that through religious activities, spirituality was significant to these students and to achieving their purpose in life. Most of the students were observed to identify one special person in their lives who is critical and important for their survival and their success. These students also believed that whatever comes their way, they can handle it through the grace of a higher being. Religion and spirituality are the driving force in most African American homes.

Participant 1 stated:
> "I believe in God. I was baptized Catholic but I do not attend church."

Participant 2 stated:
> "Most definitely. I am a Christian. I am an Episcopalian."

Participant 3 stated:
> "Ah.. I believe in God. But I wouldn't say that I am the most religious person. Ah..I am more of a spiritual person. Religion is more about having to do with believing in a structure organization of faith but spirituality is more like having faith in God but being more flexible. I wouldn't say flexible--that's wrong. I guess this is all my opinion. I am not saying that is wrong; I pray and I have morals and try to follow the right way. But at the same time I don't think I have to go to church and have to, you know, ah... formally believe in the structure like the Catholic church or Protestant church to know that I am doing well. I am a Christian."

Participant 4 stated:
> "Oh….yes sir, I am very much a religious person. I am a latter day saint, a Mormon, but my God has brought me through many trials and has gotten me in the position I am in today and so, yes, I am deeply spiritual person."

Participant 5 stated:
> "Oh yes..ah…yes…ah my grandmother brought me up in the church. Ah.. I went to a church near the convention

center called St. Stephens Baptist Church on M street. Now we moved to Temple Hills; now it is further out now but she brought me up in the church. It's kind of where a lot of my strength comes from knowing that I can pray to God ah.. for anything. It kind of get me through these times. Ah…I don't really want to go to these classes and just be the odd person in the sitting in the room. But ah…you know just the strength of God and God's love for me and the ways He has allowed me to grow and prosper just keep me going and that… yah."

Participant 6 stated:

"I do. Ah….I have a deep faith in God. Ah… I am Baptist and so you know, unfortunately, when I am living on campus, I don't get to go to church as much as I like to but, you know, when I am home during the summer I usually go with my grandmother every Sunday. Ah.. and so, but I mean, I feel like ah.. you know, when times get tough on campus or just in life as general, I feel like you know, having both that deep faith and that opportunity to reflect internally is very helpful."

Most Black men have experienced the presence of a super power in their lives. Society has labeled them as no good and out for nothing. All of the participants expressed that they are fully involved with the presence of the Lord in their daily lives. They expressed their thankfulness to the God for bringing them so far in their lives to be admitted at a predominantly White private institution of higher learning to obtain their various degrees.

Theme 9: Dealing with and Overcoming Frustration

As stated by Delgado (1998), the predominantly White Institutional model deals with the individuals who were academically capable of meeting the standards set by Whites, for example standard test scores and high-grade point averages. These are people who have assimilated culturally into the mainstream/limelight of the society and these are also the people who have the financial resources to pay for the increasing costs of education. Consequently, any individual who does not meet the standards set by the tenets of the dominating paradigm in America might have to struggle a lot at the White institutions. This has led to an increasing emotion of frustration which turns out to be detrimental for Black male students at PWIs. By removing the standards created by Whites, for example, high academic scores, test scores and high-grade averages, accepting those Black male students who have a financially strong background, can help in easing the situations and frustration faced by the Black male students at PWIs.

Participant 1 stated:
> "I am generally frustrated about kind of ah..you know, I don't mind if people choose their own social circles but I see a kind of divide between white students and black students—not anything serious—but just like social trends. There are no ill feelings about the others but black people tend to associate with black people, white people associate with white people and there is not a lot of intermingling among, there is lot of black

students that hang with white students but there is a big population of black students that only hang out with black students. It is a little frustrating, I think it could be ah..a little more diverse. I think it will add to the experience. If you go to an institution like this, you know, it is great to have a black population. It is something that I am very thankful for because I didn't know what it would be like coming to a private white institution so I am very thankful that there are so many black people here but it's kind of strange that they only associate with each other and I am included in this as well, most of my friends are black, most of the people I associate with are black and it's kind of like not what you would expect from a university like this."

Participant 2 stated:

"Ah.. well.. if you ask anybody they will say the same old junk, for me it is a good pasttime. It is a good way to elevate any frustration or any type of bad mode I may be in. It is a good place of solace so whether in the hard days after all of my classes, after doing a little bit of homework or reading, I head over for couple of hours ah…do my work out and training regimen and things of that nature. It is good for my mind and rejuvenates me and I am able to do better in the tasks ahead. Frustration, whether it be a like, hum…a difficult day in class or a subject or topic that I am not understanding ah.. if there is a personal issue or thing of that nature…"

Participant 3 stated:

"I guess maybe the professors--some of them, not all of them. I will say one in particular is my economics professor. He is very strict when it comes to certain things like ah… To a point like this didn't happen to me like say if you were sick like this girl last semester was sick with a kidney infection and missed a quiz and she wasn't given a chance to take the exam. She said that it was in the syllabus that you can't miss this bla, bla, bla, but at the same time this person could have died. Why would you do that? So I guess that will be my previous frustration and also I got ah.. you have to get twenty out of twenty-five to receive ten percent of your grades in the class and, if you don't, then you will lose ten percent of your grade and ah I didn't. She gave us four different attempts, but the last attempt, I got nineteen out of twenty-five and the only reason why I could have gotten a twenty because instead of putting like, you have to state the units right and so it was like a math problem, I wrote , I got the number right like twenty units squared but I didn't look at it properly and the units in centimeters, so I put twenty unit square and the correct answer was twenty centimeters square so when I talked to her, she said oh..well no you can't do that but if I understand the concept shouldn't that mean that, you know, that will prove that I at least deserve that and but I mean, other than that, that's okay but I know, she is just a freshman teacher and I earnestly should have consulted students before me because I would have figured out that she's not the best teacher for that class. Someone else would have been, so that will be my frustration. To overcome my frustration, first I would have looked at the question and also I guess, overall, I just have to know which professors that I am going to have in the future because, I mean, it is not all just about having easy professors but having one that is understanding and knows that we are human and everyone makes their different mistakes but that doesn't mean that you should be punished like that."

Participant 4 stated:

"Ah..I mean there is one group of kids. I don't want to call anyone's name but just the way they carry themselves and are sometimes disrespectful and they are a group of black guys. Ah..they sort of disrespect. Not what they represent but how they represent themselves. I know them individually. I am frustrated about their drinking. Some of the students drink a lot. As a student staff on the dorm, only white students have given me some hard times in representing their student IDs. I have to call security to resolve the situation."

Participant 5 stated:

"Ah…my frustration is just the lack of …lack of diversity on the campus and I don't like when ah..the university says we are very diverse student body with over thirty percent ah..multicultural and then ok..you look at the statistics they say over thirty percent but then there like is a good twenty-five percent are Asians and then everybody else is left in the five percent. Ah.. that is something that is very frustrating ah.. it's just like you advertise it as 'this is a diverse body of people' and, you know, you impress everybody and things like that and you get here and that's not how it is..ah...the brochures kill me. Like I hate the brochures because when you open the brochures everybody's having lunch together and, no, that's not how it is and you see a group of white people and just one black person in the middle and then like that. Yes, you're fooling the people about what exactly going on... ah..because we are not in a closed campus. Everybody is walking down the streets so you don't know who are actually the students until you get in the classroom. Ah.. until you actually see the composition of especially like the freshman classes are larger. I took a political science class in that class of two eighty five students and fifteen were a minority. I was shaken to walk in the classroom and then I was thinking maybe this is the first day, they will come. Ah..and then after the first week, second week and later in the semester, they didn't come and I said ok...this is it. They are not coming. I overcome my frustration by just dealing with it. I became more social in the community. The SanMag Cultural Student Services center is the saving grace and seeing another black face, I say. Ah.. I can make it and then I am charged again."

Participant 6 stated:

"Ah...I think that...I guess one of the most frustrating things on campus is just the rigor of work. You know, that I have ah..so you know, I think again having you know, a good support system on campus whether it be, you know, administrator or mentor or just friends ah..I think that it's very important ah..and you know, I really have found a very positive outlet for my frustration but I found ways to just kind of relax and take my mind out of things and just kind of go back to it when, you know, when I find the energy to ah.. so...ah...so I think just finding those outlets is one way I try to overcome frustrations."

Among participants in the study, frustrations were expressed in many ways. They are frustrated with the social circles, rigor of studies, with their professors, with certain other disrespectful Black men and the lack of diversity. Participants envisioned these frustrations when they decided to attend this predominantly White private university. They overcome these frustrations by simply finding some avenues to relax and take their minds off of any frustrating situations. Besides all of the frustrations, they are mindful of completing their college course work and getting their degrees.

Theme 10: Determination to Complete College

According to the research conducted by Howard-Hamilton (1997), they explored some of the developmental theories which could be adopted in order to fit the needs of Black male students. The study also analyzed new theories that are Afro-centric and might prove to be helpful in improving the experiences of Black men and promoting self-esteem. The study has made an effort to present a practical application of the selected theories by analyzing them. The researcher has argued that graduate faculty and practitioners need to have developmental theories that correspond accurately to the problems that are faced by Black students (Lynn, Bacon, Totten, Bridges & Jennings, 2010).

Participant 1 stated:
"Yes. I am determined to complete college."

Participant 2 stated:
"Ah.. definitely taking it one step at a time. Right now, I am stepping more into my upper biology courses, so

studying, studying, studying, repetitious, repetitious, repetitious asking questions, always reviewing, going to review classes or group review sessions—things of that nature, just to make sure that I am always on top of it and I always, like my professor that I had this last semester said, 'whenever you have a chance to read, whether it be a novel or a good text book just be reading something and keep the brain active'."

Participant 3 stated:

"Oh..definitely. I will say I am a little bit confused as to what I am going to do but ah..I know that hopefully as long as I continue to try, the outcome will be that I graduate at some point."

Participant 4 stated:

"Ah..I am determined to do whatever it takes it complete college. Even if it takes long hours. I will go to my teachers for questions that I don't understand. I will do what I have to do. I am not afraid to ask for help. To do my best. I have a 3.6 GPA and I work hard for this and I am motivated to do better. Something my mother said to me is 'Because you are black, you must strive to do your best at all times.' That statement has inspired me to always do my best to get to the next level."

Participant 5 stated:

"Ah.. failure is not an option. Ah… failure is not an option …ah..You know and so ah..you know a lot of just being on religion has just been keeping me. I don't believe that God brought me this far and I am about to be a junior now and I am just, like, He brought me through two years and I'm about to go into the third year and

> you know, He didn't bring me this far [for nothing] and He will take me to graduation. I have too many people looking up to me and ah…being the first in family to do something, I am setting the standard for future generations. Ah..and just quitting is not an option. I am just [going to] keep going and I am determined to keep moving forward to get a degree."

Participant 6 stated:

> "I am. uhm…it is difficult and ah..definitely uphill even now, halfway through, I still feel it is an uphill battle but I am very determined. Ah..I feel as though, you know, I have been given this opportunity and I have been given the money ah..and ah.. I'd be very disappointed if I couldn't complete just because I feel as though I spent a lot of time—some of it more productive than others—but I feel like I spent a lot of time you know working towards this and I spent a lot of hours dreaming, you know, about getting my degree so ah..I feel as though I am very determined to finish."

All of the participants in the study are determined to complete their college education at this university. Despite all of the obstacles in their way, they are finding various avenues to be successful at this predominantly White private university. Black men have from time to time undergone devastating hardships. These participants will join a list of other Black men that have gone through similar experiences and are now enjoying the fruit of their labor. Education for Black men is very important to improve their social and economic lives. The participants in the study are fully aware that their communities will be benefited by their contributions upon graduation from college.

Theme 11: The Importance of Social Network on Campus and the Benefits of Attending this Predominantly White Private Institution.

According to Patton (2006), students have expressed the importance of Black Culture Centers (BCC) on campuses. The physical presence of the buildings, along with the human aspects, represent recognition of Black culture, people and history. These provide positive interaction for those who visit the center.

Participant 1 stated:
> "Ah..just the Black Men Initiative is kind of like what I work for to associate and keep in contact and offer assistance, whether I am going to get this internship you had it before, you can give me pointers or this job or leadership position ah…you know, you took this class before, you can help me study and I think that's it. ah..I think that's very important. I think that no one…there are people who can survive and make it in college alone without assistance, but I think it makes the experience much more fulfilling if you have help and if you need people and if you learn how to make connections and to advance your experience."

Participant 2 stated:
> "Yes. This school has a Facebook face; also I just got into Twitter for the first time. Just to be able to link with students makes it easier to know what's happening on campus. There was a medical expo at the Smithsonian

that I was able to attend due to this school social network. Ah..yes it is very important to me. It is good way to be able to branch out and mingle with other students and to know what's going on. This past semester, actually, I started my own company; it is more like a fitness center. I want to be a body trainer after med school. I have a passion for fitness training and nutrients and things of that nature so I figure to open my own center. I have four clients this semester so definitely it will help get it off the ground."

Participant 3 stated:

"Oh yes most of them like Facebook, Twitter, Instagram. Definitely have not used them as much this first year of school. In high school, I didn't care so much about them. There have been times that I didn't go on them like days, weeks or months but ah..here I've used them every day constantly I don't [think] twenty four hours [has passed] that I haven't gone on them, which is kind of bad because it shows how you are depending on them. I guess most of the time it is for just communication to also ah..for me it is for awareness, it is supposed to be for communication, but it is almost narcissistic because you see you having fun when you doing this or that and, I don't know, I feel like I use it for myself more than using it for communicating with other people because if you want to write something funny you get lots of hits. Ah.. like something like that."

Participant 4 stated:

"Oh…yes sir. I am involved in Facebook and in the honors program on campus, I am part of the ABPsy, part of the BMI group, the MSSC group and I am part of different students groups. Ah...so they are important. I just like the honors programs. The social groups help me to keep up with individuals that I don't see often, to keep our relationship current. That's how the social network is important to me."

Participant 5 stated:

"Ah..............uh.....no. I am not as involved as I should be now which I am realizing this year so I plan to be more involved this coming school year. Ah... I have not really just ah...the...the commuting issues is the thing that kind of limits my participation on campus but I plan to do more things, especially with the alumni days and ah... trying to get more connections to the workplace because I am pretty sure that those connections will not come as easy to African Americans period, especially African American men. Those connections to these inside connections to ah.. companies is probably harder for us and that ah.. is why I probably plan to participate in more with alumni networking and things like that to try and get myself [involved] in that ah...way. It is very important. Ah....they are important because you get to talk with experienced professionals. Ah..before I decide that this [is what] I want to do with my life, I want to talk to somebody who is doing it to see if this is what I want to do. That how it is important to me to kind of solidify whether or not what I want to do with myself and that ah.. more so for my mentor--someone in my corner looking out for me. I think that is very important and it is on my list to do."

Participant 6 stated:

"Ahh...yes...yes. I think in this school students in general are very active on social media. And so, you know, kind of the networks that we create online are just as important as the networks we create kind of on campus ahh… and so you know whether, I am member of a bunch of Facebook groups, you know, different student organizations, so I mean probably about seventy five percent to eighty five percent of the events I find out about that are happening on campus, I find out on social media. Ahh.. I feel like that's the best medium so, yes, Facebook, Twitter, Instagram, any of those social media I've probably connected with this school community on all of those. Ahh…I think..ahh…I think that social media networks most specially on campus are important just because ahh...one, there is another way of communication. I feel like our community is not the largest that colleges have ever seen but there is still, you know, ten thousand undergraduates and something like that and so you know, you won't really get to meet everyone ahh...and so you know, having those outlets where ahh… you can find out about events on campus or ahh...you discuss ideas or you can ask for help or you know things like that I feel like that those outlets really help ahh… to give us access to resources that otherwise we may not find on campus just because sometimes when you are trying to find resources, sometimes you have to dig and I think that social media makes it a lot easier to do."

All of the participants expressed the benefits for matriculating to this predominantly White private institution.

Participant 1 stated:

"I have a Fullbright scholarship. I came here so I wouldn't have any debt."

Participant 2 stated:

> "Okay. I didn't want to stay in D.C. or come to this school. It was my counselor and my dad who told me to come to this school. So I filled up the school application and applied for a scholarship ah...I was going to Georgetown, I thought it half way and I decided to apply to this school. This is the only school I applied to in D.C. and lo and behold, I ended up in this school."

Participant 3 stated:

> "Ah...for starters, this is one of the best schools I [could get] into and also D.C. has always been like a city that, even though I live close by, I don't ever really explore D.C. and I know it is such a great city with amazing opportunities to do things all year round and that's definitely the main reason why I decided to come here because ah.. . just right now, I have an internship in D.C. and the fact that I can just work year round here and get to connect compared to if I would have gone somewhere else far away where I had to come back and [may] not [have been] able to do that. I come here and everything has been paid [for] with the people already living here enabling me to get something and so it is the main reason and also it is a good school."

Participant 4 stated:

> "So..actually I only applied to two different schools. My financial situation in high school wouldn't allow me to apply to many schools because I didn't have enough money for application fees. Because my dad works at this university, ah..I couldn't qualify for any aid. I applied to NYU and here. I got rejected at NYU and got accepted here. Because my dad works here I get the

student employee tuition benefit ah..you know this was a best decision for me to make and I know that this school is a good school and it is here in the city. I know that this is a predominantly white university. I am always comfortable around white people and most of my friends are white. Ah.. yes, that's the reason I came to this school."

Participant 5 stated:

"Quite honestly, I selected this school because of the financial aid. Ah… the money was right for me to come. I applied to about eleven schools and well…ah.. lot of those schools were like Rutgers and things like that. I did not want to stay in D.C. This school is the only school I applied to in D.C. and actually the area and the closest school was in New Jersey. Ah. Yes, I like D.C. I was born and raised here but I wanted to go somewhere else. I got my financial package back and it came down to here or Morehouse. I think for the social aspect, Morehouse would have been best for me. Ah..but then I was on the fence. I did not want to be around all black people. Morehouse did not give me enough money and after I tried to get more money, this school gave me more money. I am a very cheap person. I did not to take out over thirty thousand dollars in loans to complete one year of college versus coming here and don't have to take out any loan. Everything is covered. So. Ah.. yes, no loan and school with walls is right across the street from this school. Yes, kind of, I want to stay or want to go and it was back and forth. I wanted to take a lot of classes here before I matriculated..ah.. but those classes were race based. Those are the only classes [in which] you

DATA ANALYSIS AND RESULTS   159

will find majority of blacks and I was like ok, you know, so I feel comfortable. Then when you get outside of the cultural classes, you say oh….ok this is how it really is and then you know. It is something that they don't really talk about but it needs to be discussed before somebody sign the [dotted] line, thinking it is a diverse place. I don't feel like you should have to go to a SanMag cultural center to find other multicultural students that is one reason I really wanted to go to Morehouse because I didn't want to go to a building to find people like me. I should [be] able to walk through campus or sit in a classroom that's not about race or, you know, about culture and find other people like me and that is something that is not told. I am pretty sure it is a common experience for some people. Maybe because they are kind of involved more on campus than me. Ah..yes the money was right for me to come and I was just like, 'yes, [that] sounds like that's a winner and I didn't want to get in a whole lot of debt for school. Maybe I will look for a graduate school at a Black institution. But for now, I will stay here and make it work."

Participant 6 stated:

"Ahh... I think, the first reason will be the money (laughter). So, you know, that is a very good reason. But relatively late in my college search I felt like I wanted to stay in the city ahh... just because I was very involved locally in terms of civics and politics and, you know, things like that so I felt like I wanted to stay involved here as well as being involved on campus. Ahh….so this school was a good choice ahh…. I also felt like this school was the best of both worlds in my mind because we had this city campus, you know, city-based campus here with so much access, you know the White House is a few blocks away, city hall is not that much farther away ahh… you know all these resources for me, especially in the field I want to go into. I major in Political Science and ahh… so that was very important. But then, you kind of have these outlets where you kind of get away from the hassle and bustle of the city so my first year, I stayed on the Mt. Vernon campus which is in the city but you know, kind of tucked away, ahh…you know, there is grass and animals (laughter) and deer and what not ahh… and so that is also a more closed campus than this one and that was what I wanted when I envisioned college — kind of a closed campus with, you know, kind of everything kind of close together ahh…so having that experience to live on the Mt. Vernon campus my freshman year was very good. It really gives me the experience that I wanted while this campus is giving me the experience that I needed. Ahh…so I thought that was a very, I thought that was a plus in my choice for this school. Ahh… and then I feel like, you know, in terms of extra curriculum and student life, I don't think I can ask for a much better experience than with this school with the extra curriculum activities and whatever extra curriculum I want, I can probably find here ahh…. the diversity and also the ahh…the support system that the administrators give here ahh…because I feel like you know, some colleges are very corporate, very business-oriented but so think what you want about this school. But I feel like the administrators really care about the interest of the students from deans to professors to ahh…people in the multicultural student services center to other places on campus. I feel like there is a genuine affinity towards students and so I feel like if there is anything I need on campus, I can go and I know someone that I can ask and that's very good for me."

At this predominantly White private institution, there is a network provided to students called Black Men Initiatives (BMI). This network empowers them to stay focused, meet with other upperclassmen, encourage them to form study groups, obtain advice and it drives positive awareness for their academic success. Every participant expressed their appreciation for this program. All of the participants in the study showed their appreciation for social networking on campus. They utilized the SanMag cultural center, Black Men Initiative, the university Facebook page, Twitter and Instagram to keep connected to fellow classmates and friends. Social acceptance is part of the retention characteristics as stated by Vincent Tinto in his model of student retention. When students are accepted socially, they tend to feel valuable among their peers. When they are valued, they tend to remain in school. All of the participants appreciate the financial benefits received for matriculation to this predominantly White private institution.

What condition or factors contribute to the retention of first year Black male students at predominantly White private institutions?

Table 3: Cross-Participants Analysis Display

Participant	Positive Interactions with High School Teachers or Guidance and Mentors Assistance for College Preparation	Parents and Family members encouragement and support to attend college	Involvement with retention programs on campus	Student involvement	Dealing with and overcoming frustration on campus	Determination to complete college	Religion and Spirituality	The importance of social network on campus and the benefits for attending this PWPI.
1	Yes	Yes	I am a member of the Black men initiative	I attend heavily the Black student union activities	I am generally frustrated about a kind of divide between White and Black student"	Yes. I am determined to complete college	I believe in God. I was baptized Catholic but I don't attend church	Ah…I think that's very important. I have a Fullbright scholarship.
2	"Yes, most definitely"	"Yes Sir. Hum…I didn't have any choice"	With the Black Men Initiative (BMI) meeting"	I devote my time to music.	Ah…well if you ask anybody they will say the same old junk, for me it is a good pasttime	Ah…definitely taking it one step at a time	Most definitely. I am a Christian. I am an Episcopalian.	Ah…yes it is very important to me. I got good scholarship money.
3	We had one and he was very active.	Yes definitely	Oh yes…Oh yes.	I participated in film.	I guess maybe the professors	Oh…definitely	Ah…I believe in God.	Oh yes and scholarship
4	Ah…I did	They did.	With BMI	I am a member of ABPsy.	Ah…I mean there is one group of kids, Black guys.	Ah…I am determined.	Oh…yes sir.	Ah…so they are important and scholarship.
5	We had a counselor who was like a scholarship person.	Yes	With BMI	With the SSSC	Lack of diversity on the campus	Ah… failure is not an option	Oh yes..ah… yes	Those connections to these inside connections and scholarship.
6	Ah…yes	Ah… yes my mom.	Ah…I am a member of the Black Men Initiative	In the student association	Just the rigor of the work.	I am very determined.	I do. Ah…I have a deep faith in God.	Ah…yes and the money.

Summary of Themes

This chapter presented eleven themes that emerged for the data. The eleven themes were derived from both pre-collegiate and collegiate factors of the participants. These themes were the themes answering the research question: Although chapter four identified eleven themes, there are eight major themes that answered the research question - **What condition or factors contribute to the retention of first year Black male students at predominantly White private institutions?** These eight themes were observed during the second level of data analysis after reading and paying close attention to participants' responses. Riessman (2008) explains how analysis interprets and compares biographies as they are compared in the research interviews. After the process, the researcher zooms in on identifying underlying assumptions. In order to illustrate general patterns, range, and variation, assumptions of various cases are compared (Riessman, 2008). The eight themes that emerged from the study were: a) positive interactions with high school teachers or guidance and mentor assistance for college preparation, b) parents and family members' encouragement and support to attend college, c) involvement with retention programs on campus, d) student involvement, e) religion and spirituality, f) dealing with and overcoming frustration on campus, g) determination to complete college and h) the appreciation of social networks on campus and the benefits of attending this predominantly White private institution. These themes served as a basis for discussion in chapter five. These themes resulted from the interviews that were recorded in the form of narratives. These themes will also provide the readers with a better understanding of how first year Black male students can achieve academic success at a predominantly White private institution.

The participants in the study indicated that dealing with teachers or guidance helped them tremendously in regard to college readiness. By interacting with teachers on a daily basis to understand subjects being taught in college level courses, this made them realize the rigor of work ahead after high school. Mentor assistance for these participants in the study for college preparation was beneficial to them. They expressed appreciation for assistance given to them by their mentors and counselors. They finally realized that it takes a lot of preparation to enroll in college.

Parents play an important role in motivating their children to attend college. The constant reminder that you must go to college after high school is prevalent in every African American household. Some Black men struggle tremendously in high school. Therefore the desire to attend college is low. However, when they are placed in a college preparatory environment with assistance from high school administrators and counselors, they tend to enroll in college and become academically successful. For this study, the participants are all enrolled in a predominantly White private university and all of them live in the Washington, D.C. area. All have graduated from high schools in the Washington, D.C. area.

All of the participants in the study stressed the importance of the retention program at this private university for having the SanMag cultural Students Services Center and the Black Men Initiative retention program. They are reinforced by the accomplishments of other Black men when seminars are conducted to stress the importance of getting a college degree. They also expressed their satisfaction about having a place on campus they can visit to appreciate their ethnicity. All of the participants in the study are involved in different activities on campus. This has enabled them to have access to various organizations, with faculty members, deans and administrators that are heading or monitoring the activities. Given the opportunity to participate and be involved in those activities enhanced their social acceptance, thereby giving them a sense of belonging and increasing retention. Religion and spirituality are the driving force in most African American homes. Most Black men have experienced the presence of a super power in their lives. Society has labeled them as 'no good' or 'good for nothing.' All of the participants expressed that they are fully involved with the presence of the Lord in their daily lives. They expressed their thankfulness to God for bringing them so far in their lives to be admitted at a predominantly White private institution of higher learning to obtain their various degrees. As one of the participants said, "God's love for me and the ways He has allowed me to grow and prosper just keep me going and that… yeah.'

Participants in the study expressed frustration in many ways. They are frustrated with the social circles, rigor of studies, with their professors, with certain other disrespectful black men and the lack of diversity. Participants envisioned these frustrations when they decided to attend this predominantly White private university. They overcome these frustrations by simply finding some avenues to relax and take their minds out of any frustrating situations. Besides all of the frustrations, they are mindful of completing their college course work and obtaining their degrees. All of the participants in the study are determined to complete their college education at this university. Despite all of the obstacles in their way, they are finding various avenues to be successful at this university. Black men have from time to time undergone devastating hardships. These participants will join a list of other Black men that have gone through similar experiences and are now enjoying the fruit of their labor. Education for Black men is very important to improve their social and economic lives. The participants in the study are fully aware that their communities will be benefited by their contributions upon graduation from college. All of the participants in the study showed their appreciation for social networking on campus. They utilized the SanMag Cultural Student Services Center, Black Men Initiative, the university Facebook page, Twitter and Instagram to stay connected to fellow classmates and friends. Social acceptance is one aspect of the retention characteristics as stated by Vincent Tinto (2006), in his model of student retention. When students are accepted socially, they tend to feel valuable among their peers. When they are valued, they tend to remain in school.

Conclusion

This chapter provided evidence that the retention of first year black male students at predominantly White private institution can be improved. Participants were prepared to matriculate into college by the adequate college preparatory courses taken in high school and their interaction with their high school guidance responsible with providing them with those opportunities. All of the participants are determined to complete their college education. All are willing to overcome any obstacles that will hinder their academic success. The participants are religious and depend heavily on the guidance of God to see them through any obstacle. Participants are grateful to this predominantly White private institution for all the services and assistance that are being rendered to them for their academic success. Chapter 5 provides the recommendations and conclusion of this study.

CHAPTER FIVE:
DISCUSSION, CONCLUSIONS, IMPLICATIONS AND RECOMMENDATIONS

DISCUSSION, CONCLUSIONS, IMPLICATIONS AND RECOMMENDATIONS

Chapter five presents a summary of the study, a discussion of the findings in relevance to the current literature, perceptions from participants, conclusion, implications for practice and further research, suggestions for high school counselors to utilize, suggestions for college student affairs administration to utilize, suggestions for faculty members to utilize and recommendations. This chapter has provided a set of recommendations based on the findings for further research in regard to the conditions and factors that determined the retention of first year Black male students attending predominantly White private institutions leading to academic success.

Summary of the Study

The purpose of this study was to understand how six Black male students experience academic success at one predominantly White private institution in the Washington, D.C. area. This institution in the Washington, D.C. area is committed to the education of Black men. The institution has instituted various assistance programs to help the matriculation, retention and graduation of First year Black male students in their various academic pursuits. This study utilized three second semester freshmen and three sophomore Black male students that are in good academic standings with a GPA of at least 2.5 at this predominantly White private institution. This study was guided by the central research question: **What conditions or factors contribute to the retention of first year Black male students at predominantly White private institutions?** This study utilized twenty one interview protocol questions based on the participants' pre-collegiate and collegiate experiences to gain a better understanding of their academic success.

The findings of this study were organized around the central research question as well as analysis of the emerging themes. Holistic analysis was used in order to establish context. Lieblich, Tuval-Mashiach, and Zilber (1998) offer a model that will assist with the analysis and organization of narrative. The holistic approach takes into account the life experiences and stories of a person as a whole. The parts of the text were interpreted in the context of different parts of the narrated stories. Content focuses on what happened, why it happened, who participated in the event, all from the standpoint of the storyteller.

The participants interviewed in this study are in good academic standing. The range of the participants' cumulative grade point average at this predominantly White private institution in the Washington, D.C. area was 2.6 – 3.7. Five of the participants graduated from private high schools, one graduated from public high school, all six have various majors, two parents are married, two parents are single, one parent is divorced and one parent is a widow. Three are first generation college students and three are second generation college students. All of the participants are from the Washington, D.C. area.

Discussion of Findings

The eight major findings from the study are derived from pre-collegiate and collegiate experiences of the participants in achieving academic success. The major pre-collegiate findings were: a) positive interactions with high school teachers or guidance and mentors' assistance for college preparation, b) parents and family members' encouragement and support to attend college. Major collegiate findings were a) involvement with retention programs on campus, b) student involvement, c) religion and spirituality, d) dealing with and overcoming frustration, e) determination to complete college and f) the importance of social network on campus and the benefits for attending this predominantly White private institution.

Pre-Collegiate Findings towards Academic Success

Major Theme I: Positive Interactions with High School Teachers or Guidance and Mentors Assistance for College Preparation

Positive teacher-student relationships is evidenced by teachers' reports of low conflict, a high degree of closeness and support, and little dependency — have been shown to support students' adjustment to school, contribute to their social skills, promote academic performance, and foster students' resiliency in academic performance (Battistich, Schaps, & Wilson, 2004). Participants expressed their appreciation and the support received from teachers for college readiness. The participants in the study indicated that dealing with teachers or guidance helped them tremendously in regard to college readiness. By interacting with teachers on a daily basis to understand subjects being taught for college level courses made them to realize the rigor of the work ahead after high school.

Mentoring programs have had outstanding and positive results. Mentors can be assigned or chosen by the student. Heisserer and Parette (2002) indicate that "choosing a mentor for a student is a relatively simple concept" (p. 2). Mentors should be people with whom the students are in daily contact and who understand the challenges students face. Mentor assistance for these participants in the study for college preparation was beneficial to them. The participants acknowledged assistance by mentors and counselors and mentioned appreciation for them. The participants finally realized that it takes a lot of preparation to enroll in college.

Major Theme II: Parents and Family Members' Encouragement and Support to Attend College

As stated by Engle (2007), in 2005, 47 percent of first-generation students (compared with 43 percent of non-first-generation students) reported parental encouragement as a very important reason for attending college. All the participants in the study indicated that their parents and family members definitely encouraged them to attend college. Their parents and family members' encouragement stems from the fact that a college education for especially Black males is very important if they expect to survive in today's job market and if they wish to be successful in supporting their families and communities. Parents play an important role in motivating their children to attend college. The constant reminder that you must go to college after high school is prevalent in every African American household. Some Black men struggle tremendously in high school. Therefore the desire to attend college is low. However, when they are placed in a college preparatory environment with assistance from high school administrators and counselors, they tend to enroll in college and become academically successful. For this study, the participants are all enrolled in a predominantly White private university and all of them live in the Washington, D.C. area. All have graduated from high schools in the Washington, D.C. area.

Collegiate Findings towards Academic Success

Major Theme III: Involvement with Retention Programs on Campus

In a study conducted by Vaughn (2007), the need for selected intervention programs addressing the needs of Black male students was stressed. In this study the retention program at this predominantly White private institution is the Black Men Initiative (BMI). Five of the participants in the study stressed the importance of the retention program at this university for having the SanMag Cultural Students Services Center and the Black Men Initiative retention program. They are reinforced through the accomplishments of other Black men when seminars are conducted to stress the importance of getting a college degree. They also expressed their satisfaction in having a place on campus they can visit to appreciate their ethnicity.

Major Theme IV: Student Involvement

It is stated by Harper (2006), involvement is considered to be one of the key aspects for the success of Black male students at a collegial level. His study examines the gains (benefits) and outcomes (results) that are connected with outside class activities, especially experiences related to leadership. All of the participants in the study are involved in different activities on campus. This has enabled them to have access in various organizations, faculty members, deans and administrators that are heading or monitoring the activities. Given the opportunity to participate and be involved in those activities enhances their social acceptance, thereby giving them a sense of belonging and increasing retention.

Major Theme V: Religion and Spirituality

According to a research study conducted by Watson (2006), religion and spirituality in the lives of Black men in college are topics which are rarely covered by authors and researchers. In his research, Watson (2006) has presented practical definitions of both religion and spirituality. According to his definitions, spirituality is a belief in some animating, external force and Religion is adhering to an established system of practices and beliefs grounded under spirituality. Both religion and spirituality have been playing a significant part in the way African American male college students perceive their responsibilities. Watson identified and analyzed the role played by spirituality in African American male students' lives and how it can be used for developing their identity, helping them to develop their coping skills throughout their college experience. Watson reviewed several perspectives related to spirituality, considering them under a framework of daily practices for Black people. Watson's study was conducted consisting of 97 first year and second year Black male college-going students. Information was obtained about the students' religious and spiritual beliefs and their educational/ academic experiences. It was revealed in the findings that through religious activities, spirituality was significant to these students and to achieving their purpose in life. Most of the students were observed to identify one special person in their lives that is critical and important for their survival and their success. These students also believed that whatever comes their way, they can handle it with grace from a higher being. Religion and spirituality are the driving force in most African American homes.

Most Black men have experienced the presence of a super power in their lives. Society has labeled them as no good and out for nothing. All of the participants expressed that they are fully involved with the presence of the Lord in their daily lives. They expressed their thankfulness to God for bringing them so far in their lives to be admitted at a predominantly White private institution of higher learning to obtain their various degrees.

Major Theme VI: Dealing with and Overcoming Frustration

As stated by Delgado (1998), a predominantly White institutions model deals with the individuals who are academically capable of meeting the standards set by Whites, for example standard test scores and high-grade point averages. This includes people who have assimilated culturally into the mainstream/ limelight of the society and these are also the people who have the financial resources to pay for the increasing costs of education. Consequently, any individual who does not meet the standards set by the tenets of the dominating paradigm in America might have to struggle significantly at the White institutions. This has led to an increasing emotion of frustration which turns out to be detrimental for Black male students at PWIs. By removing the standards created by Whites, for example, high academic scores, test scores and high-grade point averages, accepting those Black male students who have a financially strong backgrounds, can help in easing the situations and frustration faced by the Black male students at PWIs.

Participants in the study expressed frustration in many ways. They are frustrated with the social circles, rigor of studies, with their professors, with certain other disrespectful Black men and the lack of diversity. Participants envisioned these frustrations when they decided to attend this predominantly White private university. They overcome these frustrations by simply finding some avenues to relax and take their minds off of any frustrating situations. Besides all of the frustrations, they are mindful of completing their college course work and attaining their degrees.

Major Theme VII: Determination to Complete College

The research conducted by Howard-Hamilton (1997) explored some of the developmental theories which could be adopted in order to fit the needs of Black male students. The study also analyzed new theories that are Afro-centric and might prove to be helpful in improving the experiences of Black men and promoting self-esteem. The study has made an effort to present a practical application of the selected theories by analyzing them. The researcher has argued that graduate faculty and practitioners need to have developmental theories that correspond accurately to the problems that are faced by Black students (Lynn, Bacon, Totten, Bridges & Jennings, 2010).

All of the participants in the study are determined to complete their college education at this university. Despite all of the obstacles in their way, they are finding various avenues to be successful at this predominantly White private university. Black men have from time to time undergone devastating hardships. These participants will join a list of other Black men that have gone through similar experiences and are now enjoying the fruit of their labor. Education for Black men is very important in the effort to improve their social and economic lives. The participants in the study are fully aware that their communities will be benefited with their contributions upon graduation from college.

Major Theme VIII: The Importance of Social Network on Campus and the Benefits for Attending this Predominantly White Private Institution

According to Patton (2006), students have expressed the importance of Black Culture Centers (BCC) on campuses. The physical presence of the buildings, along with the human aspects, represent recognition of Black culture, people and history, thus providing positive interactions for those who visit the center. At this predominantly White private institution, there is a network provided to all Black Male students called Black Men Initiatives (BMI). This network empowers them to stay focused, meet with other upperclassmen, encourages them to form study groups, obtain advice and drives positive awareness for their academic success. Every participant expressed their appreciation for this program. Most of the participants expressed the benefits for matriculating to this predominantly White private institution

All of the participants in the study showed their appreciation for social networks on campus. They utilized the SSSC, Black Men Initiative, the university Facebook page, Twitter and Instagram to remain connected to fellow classmates and friends. Social acceptance is an aspect of the retention characteristics as stated by Tinto (2006) in his model of student retention. When students are accepted socially, they tend to feel valuable among their peers. When they are valued, they tend to remain in school.

Perceptions from Participants

In addition to the major themes derived from the study, the researcher identified significant perceptions from the participants. All of the participants in this study started their college career at this predominantly White private institution, all of the participants stated that they enrolled at this institution because they were given scholarships and they didn't want to incur huge college debts when they graduate. All of the participants stated that they initially wanted to enroll in colleges outside of the Washington D.C. area as a means to leave home. However, when it came time for the economic packages, this university granted them more money for their matriculation. Although, as envisioned, the participants expressed their dissatisfaction with class participation among their classmates when it came to projects. As stated by participant 5: "However, a few of the Caucasians are not receptive to Black men or to me on campus. They don't want to be involved with you on class projects. They are all cooped up with other Caucasians. You are only involved with Black students. So.....ah...yes, it is difficult being a Black male on campus. The only place to talk and feel like you're being accepted is at the SanMag Cultural Students Services Center. So this is like a life saver. Ah....yes". Most of the White students prefer working with other Whites, leaving them to default to a minimum number of black students. They expressed their appreciation for the SanMag Cultural Student Services Center on campus. They stated it is a place that they appreciate, where they go to find solace and peace of mind toward the different conditions on campus. When the question of determination to complete college was asked, they all were enthusiastic to response with a "Yes" and definite acknowledgement derived for obtaining a college education as related to Black males in the United States of America. The first generation students are eager to complete college to help other family members, the community and to serve as role models for other Black males in the community.

During the face to face interview, the participants were very eager and expressive in answering the questions and indicated that they were happy to see the researcher on the other side of the table and this made them more determined to complete their college education. The researcher expressed to them that he had attended a predominantly White private institution in Minnesota to obtain his Master's Degree in Software Systems and is gainfully employed with a satellite broad band company and has taught computer information systems courses for four years at a private university in the Washington, D.C. area. The participants expressed that they understand the stereotypes placed on Black men in the United States of America and with the help of a higher power they determined as God, they will graduate from college and go beyond to further their studies. All of the participants expressed that their mothers and grandmothers were their motivating factors in enrolling in college and they are obligated to impress them because these are their source of strength in completing their college education.

Conclusion

Since the desegregation of schools in the United States of America, African Americans have obtained various degrees from all disciplines in their educational pursuits. African American men have succeeded at predominantly White private institutions given the necessary assistance to gain academic success. At this predominantly White private university, there is assistance in various forms available for Black male students to succeed. Realizing that Black male students are in the minority, the university provided the SanMag Cultural Student Services Center and approved the Black Male Initiative program for the retention of first year Black male students. All of the participants expressed their appreciation for having the SanMag Cultural Student Service Center (SCSSC) on campus. This predominantly White private university provided mentoring programs, encouragement of students to participate in leadership programs, student involvement and ample financial benefits to first year Black male students for matriculation. All of the participants expressed their satisfaction for the financial assistance received for matriculation and they are determined to complete their college education at this particular university. This predominantly White private university from the researcher's perspective has done a tremendous job in helping to provide academic success for first year Black male students. Although there are other areas that need to be improved like strongly enforcing diversity, the overall intentions are remarkable. From this study we have learned that the retention of first year Black male students can be improved given all the necessary assistance for their academic success. Information provided can be used by such private and public universities across the United States of America and Black male high school senior students who want to attend those universities for their academic success can attend.

This study confirmed that the retention of first year Black male students at predominantly White private institutions can be improved. There are other students in this category currently at other such institutions around this country. However, their stories of achievement are rarely solicited. As stated by Harper (2012), no one is a better source of instructive insights on what it takes for Black men to succeed in college than Black men who have actually succeeded in college. According to the Chronicle of Higher Education (2008), African American men and boys, on the whole, have struggled in their educational pursuits throughout American history. They graduate from high school and attend and complete college at disproportionally low rates. In higher education attendance they are outnumbered by African American women by a ratio of nearly two to one (National Center for Educational Statistics, 2008). Additionally, Harper (2008) found that fewer than a third of African American men who enter four-year colleges as freshmen graduate within six years, the lowest six year graduation rate among all racial and ethnic groups. This study was directed to the factors and conditions that contribute to the retention of six Black male students at a predominantly White private institution in the Washington, D.C. area. This study can be used by Black males graduating from high school, high school guidance counselors, retention coordinators, college administrators and faculty members in their various high schools and universities for the academic success of first year Black male students.

The participants in the study indicated that dealing with teachers or guidance helped them tremendously in regard to college readiness. By interacting with teachers on a daily basis to understand subjects being taught for college level courses enabled them to realize the rigor of work ahead after high school. Mentor assistance for these participants in the study for college preparation was beneficial to them. They expressed appreciation for assistance given to them by their mentors and counselors. They finally realized that it takes a lot of preparation to enroll in college.

Parents play an important role in motivating their children to attend college. The constant reminder that you must go to college after high school is prevalent in most African American households. Some Black men struggle tremendously in high school. Therefore the desire to attend college is low. However, when they are placed in a college preparatory environment with assistance from high school administrators and counselors, they tend to enroll in college and become academically successful. For this study, the participants are all enrolled at a predominantly White private university and all of them live in the Washington, D.C. area. All have graduated from high schools in the Washington, D.C. area.

All of the participants in the study stressed the importance of the retention program at this university for having the SanMag Cultural Students Services Center and the Black Men Initiative retention program. They are reinforced through the accomplishment of other Black men when seminars are conducted to stress the importance of getting a college degree. They also expressed their satisfaction in having a place on campus they can visit to appreciate their ethnicity. Five out of six participants in the study are engaged or were engaged in leadership roles on campus. All of them seem to enjoy the responsibilities they inherited and performed their tasks to the best of their abilities. These roles enabled them to meet other students around campus and interact with them to accomplish a designated task. Their visibility was appreciated by other racial groups on campus. Although only three participants in this study are participating in the mentoring program, they have benefitted significantly from the program and are willing to become mentors to incoming freshmen. All of the participants in the study are involved in different activities on campus. This has enabled them to have access to various organizations, faculty members, deans and administrators that are heading or monitoring the activities. Given the opportunity to participate and be involved in those activities enhances their social acceptance, thereby giving them a sense of belonging and increasing retention. Religion and spirituality are the driving forces in most African American homes. Most Black men have experienced the presence of a super power in their lives. Society has labeled them as no good and out for nothing. All of the participants expressed that they are fully involved with the presence of the Lord in their daily lives. They expressed their thankfulness to God for bringing them so far in their lives to be admitted at a White private institution of higher learning to obtain their various degrees. As one of the participant said, "God's love for me and the ways He has allowed me to grow and prosper just keep me going and that… yeah'.

Participants in the study expressed frustration in many ways. They are frustrated with the social circles, rigor of studies, with their professors, with certain other disrespectful black men and the lack of diversity. Participants envisioned these frustrations when they decided to attend this predominantly White private university. They are overcoming these frustrations by simply finding some avenues by which to relax and take their minds off of various frustrating situations. Besides all of the frustrations, they are mindful of completing their college course work and obtaining their degrees. All of the participants in the study are determined to complete their college education at this university. Despite all of the obstacles in their way, they are finding various avenues to be successful at this particular private university. Black men have from time to time undergone devastating hardships. These participants will join a list of other Black men that have gone through similar experiences and are now enjoying the fruit of their labor. Education for Black men is very important in order to improve their social and economic lives. The participants in the study are fully aware that their communities will be benefited through their contributions upon graduating from college. All of the participants in the study showed their appreciation for social networking on campus. They utilized the SanMag Cultural Students Services Center, Black Men Initiative, the university Facebook page, Twitter and Instagram to keep connected to fellow classmates and friends. Social acceptance is one of the retention characteristics as stated by Vincent Tinto (2006) in his model of student retention. When students are accepted socially, they tend to feel valuable among their peers. When they are valued, they tend to remain in school.

The retention of first year black male students at a predominantly White private institution can be improved. Participants were prepared to matriculate into college by the adequate college preparatory courses taken in high school and their interaction with their high school guidance counselors responsible with providing them those opportunities. All of the participants are determined to complete their college education. All are willing to overcome any obstacles that will hinder their academic success. The participants are religious and depend heavily on the guidance of God to see them through any obstacle. This is evidence that the retention of first year Black male students at a predominantly White private institution can be improved, given educational and financial opportunities to achieve academic excellence. However, the desire to succeed depends solely on the individual student. Tinto's (2006) model of student success addressed the fact that, given all necessary assistance to aid students' retention, it is the responsibility for each student to exercise his or her desire to succeed. As an African proverb goes "you can lead the cow to the river, but you cannot force it to drink the water." Therefore, as this study has provided the success stories of these six first year Black male students at one predominantly White private institution in the Washington, D.C. area, it is the researcher's hope that this study will empower Black Males graduating from high schools around the country that want to attend such private institutions to obtain their college degrees that they will utilize this study to their advantage for their academic success.

Implications for Practice

DISCUSSION, CONCLUSIONS, IMPLICATIONS AND RECOMMENDATIONS

The purpose of this study was to understand how six Black male students experience academic success at one predominantly White private institution in the Washington, D.C. area. The researcher is providing suggestions to high school counselors, college administrators, faculty, and for future studies. All of the suggestions provided from the findings of the study are targeted to one predominantly White private institution in the Washington, D.C. area. Therefore it is limited to this institution.

Suggestions for High School Counselors to Utilize

Based on the findings of the study the following suggestions are for high school counselors to utilize.

1. Black male students that run the risk for dropping out should be identified and provided assistance for retention.
2. Counselors should take the initiative to observe those that are at risk for dropout.
3. Counselors should always be available to render assistance to Black male students when they are requested.
4. Counselors should acknowledge all efforts made by Black male students to successfully pass their courses.
5. Counselors should put Black male students in college preparatory courses to prepare them for college readiness.
6. Counselors should encourage Black male students to participate in leadership programs.

Suggestions for College Student Affairs Administrators to Utilize

As stated by Harper (2013), Black male students are outnumbered at most colleges and universities, their grade point averages are among the lowest of all undergraduate students, their engagement in classrooms and enriching out-of-class experiences is alarmingly low, and their attrition rates are comparatively higher than those of White students in U. S. higher education (p. 3).

1. Start with Standards

As stated by Harper (2013b), in recent years, educators have employed a range of efforts to reverse problematic trends among minority male students. These activities have been disproportionately social, focusing on entertaining men of color and creating unity among them. Although it is important to offer safe spaces for these students to socialize in many campus contexts, initiatives that focus on academics, student development, and improving campus climate are also needed. Most minority male campus initiatives are arguably ineffective because they were created and launched in the absence of standards. Well-intentioned educators attempted to do something in response to a problem, but had little guidance for design and assessment. Therefore, standards should be taken in consideration when minority male initiatives are launched. This predominantly White private institution has done well in establishing standards. This university approved the Black Men Initiative (BMI) program geared toward empowering Black men to enforce academic success.

2. Recognize They Are Not All the Same

As stated by Harper (2013c), a justifiable emphasis on Black male undergraduate students has overshadowed the educational needs and experiences of their same-race female peers and other male students of color. Since 2001, more than 70 peer-reviewed journal articles and at least a dozen books and reports on Black undergraduate men have been published. Therefore, recognizing that their same-race female peers are not the same will help to eradicate attrition among Black male students on campus. This predominantly White private university is very much aware of this program and has established pairing up upperclassmen to underclassmen to strengthen the bonds of brotherhood.

3. Remember They, Too, Are Men

In *College Men and Masculinities: Theory, Research, and Implications for Practice*, Harper and Harris (2010) synthesized decades of research from education, sociology, gender studies, anthropology, and other academic disciplines. Several studies of gender differences among undergraduates highlight numerous problematic attitudinal, behavioral, and developmental trends among male students. Researchers have attributed many of these differences to gender socialization generally and troubled masculinities in particular. Interestingly, institutional activities introduced in recent years to improve the status and experiences of minority male students typically neglect to understand them as men; race is often the sole focus of institutional programming. Black men should be treated as men in the same manner White men are treated for the psychological state of Black men on campus. This predominantly White private institution is fully aware that all Black male students must be treated with similar respect as their White counterparts.

4. Seek Inspiration, Not Replication

In *African American Men in College,* Cuyjet (2006) presented nine exemplary programs and initiatives that showed promising results in improving Black male student engagement and achievement. Student affairs administrators can learn much from programs and activities that have proven effective elsewhere. Nonetheless, it is important to recognize how different campus cultures, resources, institutional norms and politics, and student characteristics may affect the implementation and success of a minority male initiative. Student affairs professionals should be mindful of the specific contexts and unique cast of local actors involved in the development of award-winning, nationally recognized programs. Just because something worked well on one campus does not mean that mere replication will produce similar results elsewhere—even in a similarly sized or geographically proximal institution. Instead of merely duplicating "model programs" or "best practices," colleagues should seek to understand the personal and institutional philosophies, planning, collaborative partnerships, intentionality, and revisions that made these initiatives successful. This predominantly White institution has adopted the model of the Black Male Initiative at Texas Southern University because it has been effective with mentoring first year Black male students resulting to retention and graduation.

5. Form Consortia and Alliances

As stated by Harper (2013 d), racial and gender inequities are too pervasive; explanatory factors for underachievement, disengagement, and attrition are too complex; and the learning curve for educators is too steep for an institution to improve the condition of college men of color on its own. Collaboration, both within and beyond the borders of a single campus, is necessary. Examples of institutions uniting for knowledge sharing and collective strategizing include: The African American Male Initiative; the Black Male Initiative, sponsored by the City University of New York; and the African-American Male Initiative, sponsored by the University System of Georgia. Each of these state and system initiatives holds an annual conference that brings together faculty, academic affairs administrators, student affairs professionals, undergraduate students, and other stakeholders. Throughout the year, they also use electronic resources to address pressing problems concerning male students of color. Therefore, forming consortia and alliances will definitely improve the retention efforts of Black men to achieve academic success. This predominantly White private university has formed consortia with Student African American Brotherhood Organization (SAAB) Program, The Morgan MILE, Morgan State University program, First year learning team (FlighT) Program conducted by Southeast Missouri State University and Glendale Community College program.

Suggestions for Faculty members to Utilize

1. Since a majority of faculty members at predominantly White private institutions are White, faculty members should have an open door policy and give Black male students equal access to them at all times. Black male students will appreciate the equal time given to them and feel accepted mentally.
2. Faculty members must give Black male students opportunities to express themselves on topics represented in class and must encourage their collaboration in various team projects with other White classmates. As stated by participant 5, "However, a few of the Caucasians are not receptive to Black men or to me on campus. They do not want to be involved with you on class projects. They are all cooped up with other Caucasians. You are only involved with Black students…" The grouping together of all Black students on a project presents division among the students.
3. Faculty members should encourage diversity and should make it their responsibility to always express to their students the importance of diversity. Participant 5 expressed his frustration with the lack of diversity on campus. As he stated: "Ah…. my frustration is just the lack of diversity on the campus and I don't like when Ah…the university says we are a very diverse student body with over thirty percent Ah.. multicultural and then..Ok.. you look at the statistics they say over thirty percent but then there like a good twenty-five percent as Asians and then everybody else is left in the five percent."
4. Faculty members must attend diversity seminars, workshops and conferences.
5. Faculty should take into consideration the various economic situations that Black male students face and must value their persistence in achieving academic success. All of the participants are determined to complete their various degrees at this predominantly White private university.

Recommendations for Further Research

This study presents recommendations for further research regarding the retention of First year Black male students at predominantly White private institutions towards their academic success. This study used a qualitative design, specifically narrative inquiry, as a method of inquiry. A replication of this study is recommended focusing on the retention of first year White male students at HBCU (Historically Black Colleges and Universities), focusing on the retention of first year Native American male students at predominantly White or HBCU (Historically Black Colleges and Universities) and focusing on the retention of first year Latino male students at predominantly White or HBCU (Historically Black Colleges and Universities). According to Ohio State University (2013), first year retention for African American students is at a record high. The first year retention rate rose three points last year to 91 percent, a record high. The national average is 85 percent for highly-selective schools as reported by the Consortium for Student Retention Data Exchange. Similarly, the rate for Hispanic students returning for their second year of study improved one point to 93 percent, topping the national mark of 86 percent. The success that Ohio State University is now experiencing is a direct result of the commitment of faculty and staff to develop high standards of teaching and great programs for students that are enrolled with challenges.

Research should also focus on the relationship between faculty and Black male students in achieving academic success at predominantly White private or White public institutions. Research questions should focus on faculty ability to notice Black male students' problems in class and be able to render assistance toward academic success. As stated by Childs (2011), further recommendations that can be used to address the retention problem among African American students and faculty should be 1) provide mandatory diversity awareness training for faculty and staff 2) offer faculty of color more incentive to work at predominantly White institutions 3) the diversity officer should have a bigger role in the hiring of more diverse faculty and staff 4) increase publicity of the African American Cultural Center along with its resources and programs for students 6) set aside money to pay for these programs, or apply for more grants that can be used to support them. This predominantly White private university is aware of its diversity problem and is taking steps to improve diversity on campus. Diversity week programs have been implemented. The SanMag Cultural Students Services Center is providing mentoring activities for first year Black male students. Grants are given to first year Black male students for matriculation and services are provided for retention. Further research should look into the practices of this particular university that have aided in the academic success of first year Black male students. This will definitely add to the literature for first year Black male student retention.

Some African Proverbs on Education by Dawn Denton (2013)

Learning expands great souls.
By crawling, a child learns to stand.
It is one word of advice that one needs to give to a wise man, and that word keeps multiplying in his mind.
He who learns, teaches.
Only God generates, man only educates.
Instruction in youth is like engraving in stone.
You always learn a lot more when you lose than when you win.
Some will learn through pain and sorrow, others through joy and laughter, so it is written.
If you think education is expensive, try ignorance.
What you learn is what you die with.
He who does his work properly has been well advised.
To get lost is to learn the way.
Listening is the most difficult skill to learn and the most important to have.

Some Photos Gallery of Educational Accomplishments

This is the joy every parent feels when one of their children graduates from college or university. One of my sons, Arnold Magnus Wilson, shared laughter after his graduation from Virginia Tech with a Bachelor's Degree in Aerospace Engineering.

DISCUSSION, CONCLUSIONS, IMPLICATIONS AND RECOMMENDATIONS 213

This is one of my sons, Seborn Nathaniel Yancy, III during his graduation ceremony at Concordia University in Saint Paul, Minnesota. He graduated with a Bachelor's Degree in Sport Management. He later went on to receive his Master's Degree.

Congratulatory handshake from Dr. David Erekson, President,
Argosy University, Washington D.C. Campus

DISCUSSION, CONCLUSIONS, IMPLICATIONS AND RECOMMENDATIONS 215

After I was hooded and now Dr. Sandy Woodrow Yancy, Sr.

I am with my wife, Magdalene Dennis Yancy after the graduation ceremony. She is wearing my hat as a sign of support she rendered during my journey.

REFERENCES

American Council on Education, (2006), *Federal student loan debt: 1993 to 2004.* Retrieved from http://www.acenet.edu/programs/policy

Artze-Vega, Isis, (2012), "The Relationship between Student Ratings and Student Retention", *Open Access Dissertations.* Pp. 785

ASHE-ERIC. (2004), Exemplary student retention programs, *Higher Education Report, 30(3),* 53-66

Astin, A.W. (1984). *Student involvement: A developmental theory for higher education. Journal of College Student Personnel, 25(2),* 297-308.

Audrey J. J. and M. Kevin Eagan, Jr (2009), *Unintended Consequences: Examining the Effect of Part-Time Faculty Members on Associate's Degree Completion Community College Review* January 2009 36: 167-194, doi:10.1177/0091552108327070

Axelson, R. D., & Flick, A. (2011). Defining student engagement. *Change, 43,* 38-43. doi:10.1080/00091383.2011.533096

Bailey, D.E., & Moore, J.L., III. (2004), Emotional isolation, depression, and suicide among African American men, Reasons for concern, In C. Rabin (Ed.) *Linking lives across borders: Gender sensitive practice in international perspective* (pp. 186-207). Pacific Grove, CA: Brooks/Cole.

Bandura, A. (1977). *Social Learning Theory*. New York: General Learning Press. Retrieved from:

learning-theories.com/social-learning-theory-bandura.html

Barefoot, Betsy, (2000). *The first year experience: Are we making it any better?* About Campus, January/February 2000, Pp. 12-18

Battistich, Schaps, & Wilson (2004). *The contribution of positive teacher-student relationships on school adjustment and academic and social performance. Retrieved from:* apa.org/education/k12/relationships.aspx

Bean, J. (1990). *Why students leave: Insights from research.* InD. Hossler, J. P. Bean, &

Bean, J. P. (1985). Interaction effects based on class level in an explanatory model of college student dropout syndrome, *American Educational Research Journal*, 22, 35-64

Bell, J, (2010), *Doing Your Research Project*, Open University Press, Pp. 290

Bell, J.S., (2002). Narrative Inquiry: More Than Just Telling Stories. *TESOL Quarterly. 36 (2)* 207-212.

Benson, K. F. (2000). Constructing academic inadequacy: African-American athlete's stories of schooling. *The Journal of Higher Education, 71(2),* 223-246.*Black Male College Achievement Study.* Philadelphia, PA: University of Pennsylvania,

Bloom, L., (2002).*From Self to Society: Reflections on the Power of Narrative Inquiry,* In S. Merriam (Ed.), Qualitative research in practice: Examples for discussion and analysis. San Francisco: Jossey-Bass.

Bonner II, F. A. and Bailey, K. W. (2006).*Enhancing the academic climate for African American college men* San Francisco: Jossey-Bass. .(pp. 24-46).

Brown, C. (2006). *The impact of campus activities on African American college men*. In M.J. Cuyjet (Ed.),*African American Men in College*, San Francisco: Jossey-Bass. pp. 47-67

Caple, R.B. (1991). Editorial.*Journal of College Student Development*, 32(5), 387. Changing minds.org (2012). Retrieved from: changingminds.org/explanatins/research/sampling/purosive_sampling.htm

Carlock, D. M., & Perry, A. M. (2008), Exploring faculty experiences with e-books: A focus group, *Library Hi Tech, 26(2)*, 244-254, doi:10.1108/07378830810880342

Carter, T. (1994). Mentor programs belong in college, too. Journal of Career Planning & Employment, 5, 51-5 Center for the Study of Race and Equity in Education.

Chesson, C. E. (2009). *Brother to Brother: A narrative inquiry of African American Male experience of academic success at Colorado State University*. Retrieved from: Amazon.Com.

Childs, C (2013). *African American Student Retention*. Retrieved from: irt2.indstate.edu/ir/assets/sem/Retention1.pdf

Chronicle of Higher Education (2008). *Graduation Rates at 4-year institutions*. Retrieved from: chronicle.texterity.com/chronicle/almanac200809#pg16

Clandinin, D. J., Pushor, D. and Orr, M. A. (2007). Navigating sites for narrative inquiry, Journal of Teacher Education, 58(1), 21-35

Clandinin, D.J. & Connelly, F. M. (1994).Telling Teaching Stories. *Teacher Education Quarterly, 21(1),* 145-58

Clandinin, D.J. & Connelly, F. M. (2000).*Narrative inquiry: Experience and story in qualitative research.* San Francisco: Jossey-Bass.

Corbin, S., & Pruitt, R. (2000).*Who am I: The development of the African American male identity. In African American males in school and society: Practices and policies for effective education* .Polite & Davis Eds. New York: Teachers College Press.

Creswell, J.W. (2003). *Research design: Qualitative, quantitative, and mixed method approaches* (2nd ed.). Thousand Oaks: Sage Publications.

Creswell, J.W. (2009). *Research design: Qualitative, quantitative, and mixed method approaches* (3rded.). Thousand Oaks: Sage Publications.

Creswell, J.W. (2009). *Research design: Qualitative, quantitative, and mixed method approaches* (3rded.). Thousand Oaks: Sage Publications.

Cross, T. (2002). African-American Student Graduation Rates. *The Journal of Blacks in Higher Education,(37)7'*. Retrieved June 20, 2012 from Ethnic News Watch (ENW) database. (Document ID: 494185541).

Cross, T., & Slater, R. B. (2001). The troublesome decline in African-American college student graduation rates, Journal of Blacks in Higher Education, 33, 102-109.

Cross, W. E. (1978). The Cross and Thomas models of psychological Nigrescence. *Journal of Black Psychology, 5,* 13-19.

Cross, W. E. (1995b). *The psychology of nigrescence: Revising the Cross model.* Handbook of Multicultural counseling (pp. 93-122). Thousand Oaks, CA: Sage.

Cross, W.E. (1971). The Negro to Black conversion experience: Towards a psychology of Black liberation. *Black World*, 20, 13-27.

Cross, W.E. (1995a). *In search of Blackness and Afrocentricity: The psychology of Black identity change,* New York: Routledge, pp. 53-72

Cureton, S. R. (2009). *Something wicked this way comes*: A historical account of Black gangsterism offers wisdom and warning for African American leadership. Journal of Black Studies, 40, 347–361.

Cuyjet, M. J. (2006). *African American college men: Twenty-first-century issues and concerns.* (pp. 3-23). San Francisco: Jossey-Bass.

Cuyjet, M. J. (2006). *African American college men: Twenty-first-century issues and concerns.* (pp. 3-23). San Francisco: Jossey-Bass.

Cuyjet, M. J. (1997). *African-American men on college campuses: Their needs and their perceptions.* New Directions for Student Services San Francisco: Jossey-Bass. No. 80, pp. 5-16

Daiute, C. & Fine, M. (2003). *Researchers as protagonists in teaching and learning qualitative research. Up close and personal: the teaching and learning of narrative research.* Washington, D.C.: American Psychological Association.

Dancy II, T. E., & Brown II, M. C. (2008). *Unintended consequences: African-American male educational attainment and collegiate perceptions after Brown v. Board of Education.* American Behavioral Scientist, 51(7), 984-1003

Dancy, T. E. (2009). *Black Men on Campus: What the Media Do Not Show Us.* Retrieved from: diverseeducation.com data analysis approaches. *Qualitative Inquiry, 8(3),* 329-347

Davis, G. F. (2010). Do theories of organizations progress? Organizational Research Methods, 13, 690-709.

Davis, R (2008), Revitalizing Retention Efforts For African-American College Students At Predominantly White Institutions, Proceedings of the Allied Academies, Volume 15, Number 2,

Decock, H., McCloy, U., Liu, S & Hu, B. (2011). The Transfer Experience of Ontario Colleges who Further their Education – An analysis of Ontario's College Graduate Satisfaction Survey. Toronto: Higher Education Quality Council of Ontario

Delgado, R, (1995). *The Imperial Scholar, In Critical Race Theory, Key Writings that formed the Movement,* K. Crenshaw. (Ed.) The New Press: N.Y.

Delgado, R, (1998). *The Imperial Scholar, In Critical Race Theory, Key Writings that formed the Movement,* K. Crenshaw. (Ed.) The New Press: N.Y.

Delgado, R., and J. Stefancic. (2001). *Critical race theory*: An introduction. New York: New York University Press.

Delgado, R., and J. Stefancic. (2001). *Critical race theory*: An introduction. New York: New York University Press.

Denton, D (2013). *African Proverbs on Education.* Retrieved from: http://www.bellaonline.com/articles/art68302.asp

Denzin, N. K., & Lincoln, Y. S. (Eds.). (2011). The SAGE handbook of qualitative research (4th ed.). Thousand Oaks, CA: Sage.

Denzin, N., & Lincoln, Y.S. (1994).*Handbook of qualitative research,* Newbury Park,

Denzin, N., & Lincoln, Y.S. (2000), Introduction: *The discipline and practice of qualitative research,* Handbook of qualitative research (2n edition).Thousand Oaks, CA: Sage.

Ely, M., Anzul, M., Friedman, T., Garner, D., & Steinmetz, A.C. (1991). *Doing Qualitative Research: Circles within circles.* New York: Faler.

Engle, S (2007). *Parental Encouragement, Career and Financial Growth Motivate First-Generation Students to Attend College, UCLA Survey Reveals.* Retrieved from: newsroom.ucla.edu/portal/ucla/Parental-Encouragement-Career-7952.aspx?RelNum=7952

Engstrom, C., & Tinto, V. (2008). Access Without Support is not Opportunity. Change, 40(1), 46-50

Erickson, E. (1980). Theory of Identity Development, Retrieved from: http://www.aui.ma/old/VPAA/cads/1204/cad-course-1204-rdg- erikerikson.pdf

Flowers, J. (1998). Improving female enrollment in Tech Ed. The Technology Teacher, 58(2), 21-25

Fontana, A. and Frey, J. H. (2008). The Interview: From Neutral Stance to Political Involvement. In Denzin, N. K., Lincoln, Y. S. (2008). Collecting and Interpreting Qualitative Materials. Los Angeles: Sage Publications

Fontana, A., & Frey, J.H. (2000). The interview: From structured questions to negotiated text. In N.K. Denzin & Y.S. Lincoln (Eds.), *Handbook of qualitative research*(2nd ed.). Thousand Oaks, CA: Sage.

Fordham, S. and Ogbu, J. (1986).*Black students' school success: coping with the burden of 'acting white'. Urban Review 18(3):176–206.*

Furr, S.R. (2002). African-American students in a predominantly-White university: factors associated with retention. College Student Journal, 36(2), 188-202

Gardner, John, and Schroeder, Charles (2003), The first year and beyond. About Campus, September-October 2003

Gardner, S. K., & Barnes, B. J. (2007), Graduate student involvement: Socialization for the professional role. Journal of College Student Development, 48(4), 369-387

Geertz, C. (1973). *The interpretation of culture,* New York: Basic Books. *Generation Students to Attend College, UCLA Survey Reveals.*

Gordon, E. T., Gordon, E. W., & Nembhard, J. G. G. (1994). *Social science literature concerning African American men. The Journal of Negro Education,* 63(4), 508-531

Hamilton, J.P., (2007). Reasons African American men persist to degree completion in higher education. *In C. Brown(Ed.), Still not equal: Expanding educational opportunity in society* (pp. 177-195). New York: Peter Lang Publishing.

Harper, S. R. (2009b), Race-Conscious Student Engagement Practices and the Equitable Distribution of Enriching Educational Experiences, *Liberal Education, Vol. 95,* No. 4, aacu.org/liberal-education/le-fa09/le-fa09_Harper.cfm

Harper, S (2013). *Five Things Student Affairs Administrators Can Do to Improve Success Among College Men of Color. Retrieved from:* naspa.org/5THINGS-MARCH2013_WEB.pdf.

Harper, S. R. & Davis III, C. H. F. (2012).*They (Don't) Care about Education: A Counter narrative on Black Male Students' Responses to Inequitable Schooling.* Educational Foundation, Winter-Spring 2012

Harper, S. R. (2004). *The measure of a man: Conceptualizations of masculinity among high-achieving African American male college students.* Berkeley Journal of Sociology, 48(1), 89-107

Harper, S. R. (2005). *Leading the way: Inside the experiences of high-achieving African American male students. About Campus,* 10(1), 8-15

Harper, S. R. (2006). *Black male students at public flagship universities in the U.S.: Status, trends and implications for policy and practice.* Washington, DC: Joint Center for Political and Economic Studies.

Harper, S. R. (2006). *Enhancing African American male student outcomes through leadership and active involvement*, San Francisco: Jossey-Bass, Pp. 68-94

Harper, S. R. (2006). *Peer support for African American male college achievement: Beyond internalized racism and the burden of 'acting White.'* Journal of Men's Studies, 14(3), 337-358.

Harper, S. R. (2006).*Enhancing African American male student outcomes through leadership and active involvement*, San Francisco: Jossey-Bass, Pp. 68-94

Harper, S. R. (2006).*Enhancing African American male student outcomes through leadership and active involvement*, San Francisco: Jossey-Bass, Pp. 68-94

Harper, S. R. (2006).*Peer support for African American male college achievement: Beyond internalized racism and the burden of 'acting White.'* Journal of Men's Studies, 14(3), 337-358

Harper, S. R. (2006a).*Black male students at public universities in the U.S.: Status, trends and implications for policy and practice.* Washington, DC: Joint Center for Political and Economic Studies

Harper, S. R. (2009). *Niggers no more: A critical race counter narrative on Black Male Student Achievement at Predominately White Colleges and Universities.* International Journal Qualitative Studies in Education

Harper, S. R. (2009b).*Race, interest convergence, and transfer outcomes for Black male student-athletes.* No. 147,(pp. 29-37). San Francisco: Jossey-Bass.

Harper, S. R. (2012). *Black male students in public colleges and universities: A 50-state report card.* Washington, DC: Congressional Black Caucus Foundation.

Harper, S. R. (2012). *Black male student success in higher education: A report from the National*

Harper, S. R. (2013). *Am I my brother's teacher? Black undergraduates, racial socialization, and peer pedagogies in predominantly white postsecondary contexts.* Review of Research in Education, 37(1), 183–211.

Harper, S. R., & Harris, F., III. (Eds.). (2010). *College men and masculinities: Theory, research, and implications for practice.* San Francisco, CA: Jossey-Bass.

Harper, S. R., & Kuykendall, J. A. (2012). *Institutional efforts to improve Black male student achievement: A standards-based approach.* Change, 44(2), 23–29.

Harper, S. R., Patton, L. D., & Wooden, O. S. (2009). Access and equity for African American students in higher education: A critical race historical analysis of policy efforts. *Journal of Higher Education, 80*(4), 389-414.

Harper, S.R. & Quaye, S.J. (2007), Student Organizations as Venues for Black Identity Expression and Development among African American Male Student Leaders, *Journal of College Student Development, 48(2),* 127-144.

Harper, S.R. & Quaye, S.J. (2007), Student Organizations as Venues for Black Identity Expression and Development among African American Male Student Leaders, *Journal of College Student Development, 48(2),* 127-144.

Harper, S.R. &Wolley, M.A. (2002), For African American Undergraduate Men: Strategies for Increasing African American Male Participation in Campus Activities. *The Bulletin.*16-24

Harper, S.R., & Nichols, A.H., (2008), Are They Not All The Same?: Racial Heterogeneity Among Black Male Undergraduates. *Journal of College Student Development, 49(3),* 199-214.

Harper, S.R., & Hurtado, S., (2007), Nine Themes in Campus Racial Climates and Implications for Institutional Transformation, *New Directions for Student Services, 120*, 7-24.

Hébert, T. P. (2002). *Gifted Black males in a predominantly White university: Portraits of achievement.* Journal for the Education of the Gifted, 26, 25-64.

Heisserer, D., & Parette, P. (2002). Advising at risk students in college and university settings, College Student Journal, 36(1), 69-83

Heisserer, D., & Parette, P. (2002). *Advising at risk students in college and university settings*, College Student Journal, 36(1), 69-83

Heisserer, D., & Parette, P. (2002). Advising at risk students in college and university settings, College Student Journal, 36(1), 69-83

Howard, F. (2010). *Ohio Institutions Focus on Black Male Achievement.* Retrieved from: diverseeducation.com/cache/print.php?articleId=13597

Howard, T. C. (2008). *Who really cares? The disenfranchisement of African American males in pre K-12 schools: A critical race theory perspective.* Teachers College Record, *110*(5), 954-85

Howard-Hamilton, M. F. (1997). *Theory to practice: Applying developmental theories relevant to African American men.* (pp. 17-30). San Francisco: Jossey-Bass.

Howard-Hamilton, M. F. (1997). *Theory to practice: Applying developmental theories relevant to African American men.* (pp. 17-30). San Francisco: Jossey-Bass.

Howard-Hamilton, M. F. (1997). *Theory to practice: Applying developmental theories relevant to African American men.* (pp. 17-30). San Francisco: Jossey-Bass.

Hu, W. (2011). *Bullying law puts New Jersey schools on spot.* Retrieved from nytimes.com/2011/08/31/nyregion/bullying-law-puts-new-jersey-schools-on-spot.html?pagewanted=all

Ishitani, T. T. (2006). Studying Attrition and Degree completion Behavior among First Generation College Students in the United States. The Journal of Higher Education, 77(5), 861-885

Jackson, J. F. L., & Moore III, J. L. (2008).*The African-American male crisis in education: A popular media infatuation or needed public policy response?* American Behavioral Scientist, *51*(7), 847-853.

Johnson, V.D. (2008). Welfare Reform, Race and African American Single Mothers' College Access. Accepted for presentation to the annual meeting of the ACPA-College Student Educators International; Atlanta, Georgia; March 29, 2008.

Josselson, R. & Lieblich A., (2003). A framework for narrative research proposals in psychology, In R. Josselson, R. A. Lieblich & D.P. McAdams (Eds.), *Up Close and personal: The teaching and learning of narrative research.* Washington, D.C.: American Psychological Association.

Journal of African America Males in Education (2011), Leading Educators Series, Vol 2 Issues 1 / 2. Retrieved from: http://journalofafricanamericanmales.com/wp-content/uploads/downloads/2011/03/Jawanza-Kunjufu2.pdf

Justiz, M., (1994). Demographic trends and the challenges to American higher education. In Justiz, Wilson, and Bjork (Eds.), Minorities in Higher Education(pp. 1–21). Phoenix, AZ: Oryz Press and ACE.

Kidwell, B, Hardesty, D and Childers, T. L.,(2008), "Consumer Emotional Intelligence: Conceptualization, Measurement, and the Prediction of Consumer Decision Making," Journal of Consumer Research, 35 (June), 154–66

Kidwell, K. S., (July) Understanding the college first-year experience. The Clearing House, Vol. 78, No. 6 July/August

Kimbrough, W. M., & Harper, S. R. (2006).*African-American men at historically Black colleges and universities: Different environments, similar challenges.* San Francisco: Jossey-Bass, Pp. 189-209

King, S. H. (1993). *The limited presence of African-American teachers*, Review of Educational Research, 63(2), 115-149

Knapp, Kelly-Reid, & Whitmore, (2006): *Enrollment in Postsecondary Institutions, Fall 2004; Graduation Rates, 1998 & 2001 Cohorts; and Financial Statistics, Fiscal Year 2004.* Retrieved from: nces.gov.

Kuh, G. (2003). What we're learning about student engagement from NSSE. Change, 35(2), 24-32

Kuh, G., &Andreas, R.E. (1991). It's about time: Using qualitative methods in student life studies, *Journal of College Student Development, 32,* 397-405

Kuh, G.D. (2009). What student affairs professionals need to know about student engagement. Journal of College Student Development, 50(6), 683-706. doi:10.1353/csd.0.0099

Kuh, G.D., Kinzie, J., Schuh, J.H., Whitt, E.J., & Associates (2005/2010). Student success in college: Creating conditions that matter. San Francisco: Jossey-Bass

Lang, M. (1992). *Barriers to black's educational achievement in higher education. Journal of Black Studies, 22* (4), 510-523

Lau, L. K. (2003). Institutional factors affecting student retention. Education 124(1): 126–136

LaVant, B. D., Anderson, J. T., and Tiggs, J. W. (1997). Retaining *African American men through mentoring initiatives,* San Francisco: Jossey-Bass. Pp. 43-53

Leech, N. L., & Onwuegbuzie, A. J. (2008), Qualitative data analysis: A compendium of techniques for school psychology research and beyond, *School Psychology Quarterly, 23,* 587–604

Leedy, P. D., & Ellis Ormrod, J. (2010). Practical Research (9 ed.). Upper Saddle River, NJ: Pearson.

Leppel, K. (2002). Similarities and Differences in the College Persistence of Men and Women. *The Review of Higher Education, 25*(4), 433-450

Lieblich, A., Tuval-Mas, R. and Zilber, T. (1998).*Narrative Research,* Thousand Oaks, CA: Sage Publications.

Lieblich, A., Tuval-Mas, R. and Zilber, T. (1998).*Narrative Research,* Thousand Oaks, CA: Sage Publications.

Loo, C.M. & Rollison, G. (1986).*Alienation of ethnic minority students at a predominantly white university.* Journal of Higher Education, 57 (1), 58-77

Lyle, E., (2009), Process of Becoming: In Favour of a Reflexive Narrative Approach, The Qualitative Report Volume 14 Number 2, 293-298

Lynn, M., Bacon, J. N., Totten, T. L., Bridges III, T. L., & Jennings, M. E. (2010). *Examining teachers' beliefs about African-American male students in a low-performing high school in an African American school district,* Teachers College Record, 112(1), 289-330

Lynn, M., Bacon, J. N., Totten, T. L., Bridges III, T. L., & Jennings, M. E. (2010). *Examining teachers' beliefs about African-American male students in a low-performing high school in an African American school district,* Teachers College Record, 112(1), 289-330

Lynn, M., Bacon, J. N., Totten, T. L., Bridges III, T. L., & Jennings, M. E. (2010). *Examining teachers' beliefs about African-American male students in a low-performing high school in an African American school district,* Teachers College Record, 112(1), 289-330

Manning, K. (1992). *A Qualitative Exploration of the First-Year Experience of Latino College Students,* Retrieved from: http://journals.naspa.org/jsarp/vol40/iss1/art5/ MARCH2013_WEB.pdf

Mattern, K. D., & Patterson, B. F. (2009), Is Performance on the SAT Related to College Retention. New York: The College Board

Merriam, S. B. (2001). *Qualitative research and case study applications in education.* San Francisco: Jossey-Bass.

Merriam, S. B. (2012). *Qualitative Research: A Guide to Design and Implementation (Jossey-Bass higher & adult education series).* San Francisco: Jossey-Bass.

Mickelson, R. A., Smith, S. S. (1992). *Education and the struggle against race, class, and gender inequality,* An anthology, Belmont, CA: Wadsworth. Pp.359 – 376

Milner IV, H. R. (2007). African-American males in urban schools: No excuses—teach and empower. *Theory Into Practice, 46*(3), 239-246

National Center for Education Statistics, (2003), *Postsecondary institutions in the United States:* Washington, DC: U. S. Government Printing Office.

National Center for Education Statistics, (2006), *Postsecondary institutions in the United States: Fall 2004 and degrees and other awards conferred: 2003-04.* Washington, DC: U. S. Government Printing Office.

National Center for Education Statistics, (2008), *Postsecondary institutions in the United States: Fall 2004 and degrees and other awards conferred: 2003-04.* Washington, DC: U. S. Government Printing Office. *National marks.* Retrieved from: osu.edu/news/newsitem3301

Nealy, M. J. (2009). *Black Males Achieving More on College Campuses*, Retrieved from: www.diverseeducation.com

Nes, L., Evans, D., Segerstrom, S.(2009). Optimism and college retention: Mediation by motivation, performance, and adjustment. Journal of Applied Social Psychology, 39(8), 1887-1912

Noble, K., Flynn, N. T., Lee, J. D., & Hilton, D. (2007), Predicting Successful College Experiences: Evidence from a First Year Retention Program, Journal of College Student Retention, 9(1), 39-60

Noguera, P. (2008). The trouble with black boys and other reflections on race, equity, and the future of public education. San Francisco, CA: Wiley & Sons.

NYUWagner, (2012), *Critical Race Theory*, P11.4430, 2 points, retrieved from http://wagner.nyu.edu/courses/courseDetail.php?nbr=P11.4430

Ohio State University (2013). *Minority retention, graduation rates at Ohio State exceed National marks.* Retrieved from: osu.edu/news/newsitem3301

Ollerenshaw, J.A. & Crenshaw, J.W. (2002), Narrative research: A comparison of two restorying *Data analysis approaches. Qualitative Inquiry, 8(3), 329-347*

Osborne, J. W. (1999). Unraveling underachievement among African-American boys from an identification with academics perspective, Journal *of Negro Education, 68*(4), 555-565

Palmer, R. T., & Young E. M. (2009), Determined to succeed: Salient factors that foster academic success for academically unprepared Black males at a Black college, *Journal of College Student Retention, 10*(4), 465-482

Palmer, R. T., Davis, R. J., & Hilton, A. A. (2009), Exploring challenges that threaten to impede the academic success of academically underprepared African-American male collegians at an HBCU. *Journal of College Student Development, 50*(4), 429-445.

Pascarella, E. T., & Terenzini, P. T. (2005). How college affects students, Volume 2: A third decade of research. San Francisco: Jossey-Bass.

Pascarella, E. T., Duby, P. B., & Iverson, B. K. (1983, April). A text and reconceptualization of a theoretical model of college withdrawal in a commuter institution setting, Sociology of Education, 56(2), 88-100

Pascarella, E., & Terenzini, P. (2005) *How college affects students (Vol. 2): A third decade of research.* San Francisco: Jossey-Bass.

Patitu, C. L., & Terrell, M. C. (1997), Participant perceptions of the NASPA Minority Undergraduate Fellows Program, NASPA Journal, 17, 69-80

Patton, L. D. (2006). *The Voice of Reason: A Qualitative Examination of Black Student Perceptions of Black Culture Centers.* Journal of College Student Development.

Patton, L. D. (2006). *The Voice of Reason: A Qualitative Examination of Black Student Perceptions of Black Culture Centers.* Journal of College Student Development.

Patton, L. D. (2006). *The Voice of Reason: A Qualitative Examination of Black Student Perceptions of Black Culture Centers.* Journal of College Student Development.

Perna, L. W. (2005). The Benefits of Higher Education: Sex, Racial/Ethnic, and Socioeconomic Group Differences. *The Review of Higher Education, 29*(1), 23-52

Perna, L. W., & Titus, M. A. (2005). The Relationship between Parental Involvement as Social Capital and College Enrollment: An Examination of Racial/Ethnic Group Differences. *The Journal of Higher Education, 76*(5), 485-518

Perry, J. L. & Locke, D. C. (1985). *Career Development of Black Men: Implications for School Guidance Services.* Journal of Multicultural Counseling and Development, Volume 13, Issue 3, pages 106-111

Pfleeger, S. L., & Mertz, N. (1995). Executives mentoring: What makes it work? Communications of the Association for Computing Machinery (ACM), 28, 63-73

Picket, J.P. (2000). *The American Heritage Dictionary of the English Language.* Fourth Edition, Boston: Houghton Mifflin Company, 2000.

Polite, V.C. & Davis, J.E. (1999), *African American Males in School and Society.* Teachers College. Columbia University.

Ragin, C and Amorosa, L. M. (2011), Constructing Social Research, Sage Publications, Pp. 144-248

Ragin, C. (1994). *Constructing Social Research.*Pine Forge Press; Thousand Oaks, CA.

Rice, M. F., & Alford, B. C. (1989). A Preliminary Analysis of Black Undergraduate Students' Perceptions of Retention/Attrition Factors at a Large, Predominantly White, State Research University in the South. *The Journal of Negro Education, 58*(1), 68-81

Richards, K. (2007) A phenomenological study of African American male scholars. Ph.D. dissertation, Walden University, United States — Minnesota, Retrieved from ProQuest Digital Dissertations database, Publication No.AAT 3254442.

Riessman, C.K. (2008). *Narrative Methods for the Human Sciences.*Los Angeles: Sage Publications.

Robinson, T., & Howard-Hamilton, M. (1994).*An Afrocentric paradigm: Foundation for a healthy self-image and healthy interpersonal.* Journal of Mental Health Counseling, 16(3), 327.

Salinitri, G. (2005). The effects of formal mentoring on the retention rates for first year low achieving students. Canadian Journal of Education, 28, 853-873

Santos, S. J., & Reigadas, E. T. (2004). *Understanding the student-faculty mentoring process: Its effects on at-risk university students.* Journal of College Student Retention Research Theory and Practice, 6, 337-57

Schott Foundation for Public Education. (2010). *Yes we can: The Schott 50 state report on public education and Black males.* Cambridge, MA: Author

Scott, W. D., Dearing, E., Reynolds, W.R., Lindsay, J.E., Baird, G.L., & Hamill, S. (2008). *Cognitive self-regulation and depression: Examining academic self-efficacy and goal characteristics in youth of a Northern Plains tribe.* Journal of Research on Adolescence, 18(2), 379-394.

Seifert, T. A., Drummond, J., & Pascarella, E. T. (2006). *African-American students' experiences of good practices: A comparison of institutional type.* Journal of College Student Development, 47(2), 185-205.

Shapiro, T. M. (2004). *The hidden cost of being African American: How wealth perpetuates inequality.* New York: Oxford University Press.

Shotton, H. and Williams, R. (2011). *Indigenous Peoples knowledge community: Unpacking the issues of invisibility among Native American students.* NASPA Knowledge Communities, March 2011, 28-29

Simmons, A. B., Musoba, G. D., & Chung, C. G. (2005). *Persistence Among First-Generation College Students in Indiana: The Impact of Precollege Preparation,* College Experiences, and Financial Aid. Bloomington: Indiana Project on Academic Success.

Smart, J. C. (Ed.). (2009). *Higher Education: Handbook of Theory and Research,* Volume 24 (Vol. 24): Springer.

Smith, S. A. (2010), *A study of how predominantly white institutions of higher Education in Indiana address retention and graduation Rates of African American students,* Indiana State University, Pp. 5-98 http://scholars.indstate.edu/bitstream/10484/1530/1/Smiith,%20Shawn.PDF

Stinson, D. W. (2006). *African American male adolescents, schooling (and mathematics): Deficiency, rejection, and achievement.* Review of Educational Research, 76(4), 477-506.

Strayhorn, T. L. (2010). When race and gender collide: Social and cultural capital's influence on the academic achievement of African-American and Latino males. *The Review of Higher Education,* 33(3), 307-332.

Suen, H. K. (1983), *Alienation and Attrition of Black College Students on a Predominately White Campus,* Office of Special Projects, Northern Illinois University.

Sutton, M. E. (2006).*Developmental mentoring of African American college men.* (pp. 95-111). SanFrancisco: Jossey-Bass.

Sutton, M. E. (2006).*Developmental mentoring of African American college men.* (pp. 95-111). SanFrancisco: Jossey-Bass.

Sutton, M. E. (2006).*Developmental mentoring of African American college men.* (pp. 95-111). SanFrancisco: Jossey-Bass.

Svanum, S &Bigatti, S. M. (2006).*Academic Course Engagement During One Semester Forecasts College Success: Engaged Students Are More Likely to Earn a Degree, Do It Faster, and Do It Better.* Journal of College Student Development.

Swail, W. S., Redd, K. E., & Perna, L. W. (2003). Retaining minority students in higher education: A framework for success. ASHE-ERIC Higher Education Report, 30(2), 1-172.

The chronicle of Higher Education Almanac. (2007). *Undergraduate Grades, 2007-2008.* Retrieved from: http://chronicle.com/article/Undergraduate-Grades-2007-8/48025/

Thomas, D. E., & Stevenson, H. C. (2009). Gender risks and education: The particular classroom challenges for urban low-income African-American boys. *Review of Research in Education, 33*, 160-180.

Tinto, V. (1987), The Principles of Effective Retention. Paper presented at the Maryland College Personnel Association, Largo, MD.

Tinto, V. (2000), What have we learned about the impact of learning communities on students? Assessment Update, 12(2), 1-2, 12

Tinto, V. (2006), Research and Practice of Student Retention: What Next? Journal of College Student Retention, 8(1), 1-19

Tinto, V. (2006), *Research and Practice of Student Retention: What Next*? Journal of College Student Retention, 8(1), 1-19

Tinto, V. (2006), Research and Practice of Student Retention: What Next? Journal of College Student Retention, 8(1), 1-19

Tinto, V., (1993). *Tinto's Model of Student Retention.* Retrieved from: http://www.psy.gla.ac.uk/~steve/localed/tinto.html

Titus, M. A. (2006). Understanding College Degree Completion of Students with Low Socioeconomic Status: The Influence of the Institutional Financial Context. Research in Higher Education, 47(4), 371-398.

Toldson, I. A. (2008).*Breaking barriers: Plotting the path to academic success for school-age African-American males*, Washington, DC: Congressional Black Caucus Foundation.

U.S. Department of Education, National Center for Education Statistics, (2009).*The condition of education 2009* (NCES 2009-101), Washington, D.C.: U.S.Government Printing Office.

U.S. Department of Education.(2010). *Digest of Education Statistics, 2009*. Washington, DC: National Center for Education Statistics.

United States Census Bureau (2009), Retrieved from: http://www.census.gov/popest/data/historical/2000s/vintage_2009/

Upcraft, M., & Gardner, J. (1989). A comprehensive approach to enhancing freshman year success. In M. Upcraft & Gardner, J. (Eds), The freshman experience: Helping students survive and succeed in college San Francisco: Jossey-Bass, Pp.1-12.

Vaughn, E. L. (2007). *The Challenges of Retaining African-American Males in Higher Education,* Retrieved from: www.maricopa.edu/studentaffairs/minoritymales

Vaughn, E. L. (2007). *The Challenges of Retaining African-American Males in Higher Education,* Retrieved from: www.maricopa.edu/studentaffairs/minoritymales

Vaughn, E. L. (2007). *The Challenges of Retaining African-American Males in Higher Education,* Retrieved from: www.maricopa.edu/studentaffairs/minoritymales

Watson, L. (2006). *The role of spirituality and religion in the experiences of African American male college students*, San Francisco: Jossey-Bass, Pp. 112-127.

Watson, L. (2006). *The role of spirituality and religion in the experiences of African American male college students*, San Francisco: Jossey-Bass, Pp. 112-127.

Watson, L. (2006). *The role of spirituality and religion in the experiences of African American male college students*, San Francisco: Jossey-Bass, Pp. 112-127.

Waugh, G., & Micceri, T. (1994). Using Ethnicity, SAT/ACT Scores, and High School GPA to Predict Retention and Graduation Rates. Paper presented at the Florida Association for Institutional Research Conference.

Whitt & Kuh. (1997). *A Comparison of Student Experiences with Good Practices in Undergraduate Education Between 1990 and 1994* The Review of Higher Education – Volume 21, Number 1, Fall 1997, pp. 43-61

Yin, R. K (2008), *Case Study Research: Design and Methods*, California: Sage Publication Inc.

Zajacova, A, Scott M. L, and Espenshade, T. J. (2005), *Research in Higher Education, Vol. 46, No. 6,* 677-703, DOI: 10.1007/s11162-004-4139-z

APPENDICES

APPENDIX A

Introductory Script

Dear Participant,

I am a doctoral student in Educational Leadership at Argosy University interested in conducting my Dissertation Research on *The Retention of First Year Black Male Students at Predominantly White Private Institutions.* I attended a White private institution in St. Paul, Minnesota to obtain my Master's degree in Software Systems. I have chosen your university for my study because it is a predominantly white private institution in the Washington, D.C. area. I will appreciate your participation in my study.

You have been approached to provide your participation for the research. This study is part of a dissertation process being presented to the faculty at Argosy University. The purpose of this research is to analyse *The Retention of First Year Black Male Students at Predominantly White Private Institutions*. There are number of issues faced by Black male students when they enter college to seek higher education. The research will focus on studying the perception and attitude along with the factors that influence black male students in acquiring academic achievements. Furthermore, this study will provide voice to a small population that is often neglected or misinterpreted. Black males have a story to tell about their academic experience that is uniquely their own. It is likely different from their white colleagues and dissimilar to Black women. Research will be conducted through interviews. Before giving consent to participate in this research, kindly read the section below and ask any question if you wish to understand what your participation will involve.

Statement of Non-Retribution

At the interview, you will be advised that participation in this study will be voluntary, and that you can withdraw from this study at any time without penalty. The interview will be audio taped to ensure that I will gather all significant information.

Confidentiality

All the information you provide for this research will remain confidential, unless otherwise required by law. Otherwise, all information will be held in strict confidence and will be used only for purposes of supervision, training, and education. Your name and all identifying information will be altered to protect your anonymity and confidentiality. If you participate in this study, audio taping will occur for research purposes. These tapes will be destroyed when the material is no longer needed for data analysis. The results of this study may get published in scientific journals.

If you have any questions regarding the research or if you would like a summary of the research findings, please contact me. Thank you for your assistance with this study.
Sincerely,

Dr. Sandy Woodrow Yancy, Sr.
Argosy University
Washington, DC Campus

Appendix B

Interview Guide: Dealing with Pre-Collegiate and Collegiate Factors

Interview Guide: Dealing with Pre-Collegiate and Collegiate Factors

1. Who was your favorite teacher?
2. What impact did that teacher has on your academic success in high school?
3. How did you overcome obstacles that were hindering your study time?
4. Did you seek advice from your mentor or counselor for college preparation?
5. How did your mentor help you prepare for college?
6. How did you envision college?
7. Did your parents encourage you to attend college?
8. How did you feel when you graduated from high school?
9. Are you involved in any retention program on campus?
10. Tell me about the retention program and how has it help your retention at this university?
11. Do you get support from your family members?
12. How is the social life on campus towards black male students?
13. Are you involved in any leadership role on campus?
14. What is your participation with mentoring programs on campus?
15. What is your involvement in the different activities on campus?
16. Are you a religious person or do you believe in God?
17. Are you frustrated with any conditions on campus and what do you do to overcome your frustration?
18. How are you determined to complete college?
19. Are you involved in any social network on campus?
20. How are they important for you?
21. Why did you select this university?

APPENDIX C
ALTERNATIVE CONSENT FORM FOR RESEARCH CONTAINING HUMAN SUBJECTS

Argosy University/Washington D. C. Alternative Consent Form for Research Containing Human Subjects

Dear Prospective Participant:

My name is Sandy Woodrow Yancy and I am a doctoral student in the Education department at Argosy University-Washington, D.C. Campus working on my dissertation. This study is a requirement to fulfill my degree and will not be used for decision-making by any organization. This study is for research purposes only.

You are cordially invited to volunteer your participation in my dissertation research. The purpose of this research is to obtain a better understanding about how to retain the first year Black male students at predominantly White private educational institutions.

If you agree to be in this study, you will be asked to participate in two focus group interviews. Each interview will take approximately one to two hours. During the focus group interview, you will be asked to discuss your experiences as they relate to your pre-collegiate and post-collegiate experience by answering my interview questions.

The second focus group interview will be a mixed group of both freshmen and sophomores. During the focus groups, you will be asked to discuss your experiences around your desires to drop out or stay enrolled at this school, and you may experience distress as a result. While mental health referrals will be made in this event, the participant should be aware that the researcher cannot control either comments made by other participants during the focus group or after the focus group.

No identifying information will be collected; however this study is not entirely confidential as other members may discuss the content of the focus group interview.

What Will Be Involved If You Participate?

Your participation in this study is completely voluntary. If you participate in this research, you will be asked to complete and/or participate in two focus group interview sessions. Participants will be surveyed during the focus group conversation to learn if they are available to participate in the combined focus group session which will take place two to three days after the initial focus group session.

How Long Will This Study Take?

Each interview sessions will last approximately sixty to ninety minutes over a five day period. The research will be conducted between 11:00 a.m. and 2:00 a.m. You will be asked to participate during this timeframe. Interviews will be conducted at the Multicultural Student Center.

What If You Change Your Mind About Participating?

You can withdraw at any time during the study. Your participation is completely voluntary. If you choose to withdraw, your data can be withdrawn as long as it is identifiable. Your decision about whether to participate or to discontinue participating will not jeopardize your future relations with Argosy University-Washington D.C. or your school district. You can do so without fear of penalty or negative consequences of any kind.

How Will Your Information Be Treated?

The information you provide for this research will be treated confidentially, and all data (written and recorded) will be kept securely. Written documentation will be stored in a locked file cabinet, accessible only by me, in my home. Recorded data and transcribed data will be stored on my personal password protected laptop, which is accessible only by me, then transferred to the locked cabinet after the research is completed.

Results of the research will be reported as summary data only, and no individually identifiable information will be presented. In the event that your information is quoted in the written results, I will use pseudonyms or codes to maintain your confidentiality.

All information obtained will be held with the strictest confidentiality. You will be asked to refrain from placing your name or any other identifying information on any research form or protocols to further ensure confidentiality is maintained at all times. All recorded information will be stored securely for three years, as per Argosy University-Washington D.C. requirements. At the end of the three years, all recorded data and other information will be deleted and all written data will be shredded.

Confidentiality

All the information you provide for this research will remain confidential, unless otherwise required by law. Otherwise, all information will be held in strict confidence and will be used only for purposes of supervision, training, and education. Your name and all identifying information will be altered to protect your anonymity and confidentiality. If you participate in this study, audio taping will occur for research purposes. These tapes will be destroyed when the material is no longer needed for data analysis. The results of this study may get published in scientific journals.

What Are the Benefits in This Study?

There will be no direct or immediate personal benefits from your participation in this research, except for the contribution to the study. For the professional audience, the potential benefit of this research will provide additional knowledge to the literature on the retention of first year black male students at predominately white private institutions. You also have the right to review the results of the research if you wish to do so. A copy of the results may be obtained by contacting me at: Email: syancy@stu.argosy.edu or Phone: (703) 728-0216. Additionally, should you have specific concerns or questions, you may contact my dissertation chair, Dr. Joan Jackson at Argosy University-Washington DC, by phone at (703) 526-5860/202-277-0993 or email at joanjackson@argosy.edu, or Dr. James Sexton, IRB Chair at (703) 526-5884 Argosy University-Washington DC 1550 Wilson Boulevard, Suite 600, Arlington, VA 22209 or email at jesexton@argosy.edu.

I have read and understand the information explaining the purpose of this research and my rights and responsibilities as a participant. My signature below designates my consent to voluntarily participate in this research, according to the terms and conditions outlined above.

Participant's Signature: _____
Date: _____

Print Name: _____

(The participant should retain one of the two copies of the consent letter provided by the principal investigator.)

Appendix D
IRB Approval

IRB Approval

March 26, 2013

Argosy University, Washington D.C.

Dear Mr. Sandy Woodrow Yancy, Sr:

Your application that was initially completed on March 1, 2013, and revised on March 11, 2013 was reviewed on March 26, 2013 for Argosy University, Washington D.C. Institutional Review Board (IRB) certification for your project, "The Retention of First Year Black Male Students at Predominately White Private Institutions," Research Project Number A13-011, for the period March 27, 2013 to March 25, 2014. You may now proceed with your research project, following the protocol and modified consent form that were certified and returned with a stamp by the IRB. If you wish to continue with your study beyond March 25, 2014, a Continuing Review Form must be submitted to and certified by the IRB.

Your research must be conducted according to the protocol and consent form that were certified by the IRB. Any changes to the protocol (including changes in recruitment and recruitment materials) must be reported to and certified by the IRB before the changes may be implemented. You must report any adverse events or reactions to the IRB. **When the study is complete, you must submit a Project Completion Report in order to receive clearance for graduation** (these and other forms are available on the campus web site at argosydc.net/forms/index.php and in the future on the Campus Commons at mycampus.argosy.edu/portal/server.pt).

Please contact our office with any questions. All future correspondence must include the IRB protocol number and the title of the study.

Sincerely,

James Sexton, Ph.D.
Chair, Institutional Review Board

cc: Dr. Joan Jackson

IRB Certified

From _____3/26/13_____ To ____3/25/14_____

A13-011

Appendix E

Permission email from Dr. Vincent Tinto for using his Model of Student Retention dated January 7, 2014

Dear Sandy:

Please excuse the delay in responding to your email. Events often derail…In any case, please feel free to use the model in your dissertation.

vincent tinto

On Nov 18, 2013, at 11:05 AM, Yancy, Sandy > wrote:

Dr. Tinto,

    I am a doctoral student at Argosy University in Washington, D.C. I am pursuing my Doctorate degree in Educational Leadership. Kindly grant me the permission to use your model of student retention in my dissertation. My dissertation topic is "THE RETENTION OF FIRST YEAR BLACK MALE STUDENTS AT PREDOMINATELY WHITE PRIVATE INSTITUTIONS". Your model of student retention along with Dr. Shaun Harper Critical Race Theory Application is my theoretical framework.
    Your assistance in this request will be highly appreciated.

Respectfully,

Mr. Sandy Woodrow Yancy
Argosy University
Education Department
Washington, DC Campus

CPSIA information can be obtained at www.ICGtesting.com
Printed in the USA
BVOW02*0416170915

418115BV00003B/11/P